Praying with the Early Christians

PRAYING

WITH THE
EARLY CHRISTIANS

A Year of Daily Prayers
and Reflections
on the Words
of the Early Christians

EUGENE H. PETERSON

HarperSanFrancisco
A Division of HarperCollins*Publishers*

PRAYING WITH THE EARLY CHRISTIANS. *A Year of Daily Prayers and
Reflections on the Words of the Early Christians.* Copyright © 1994 by
Eugene H. Peterson. All rights reserved. Printed in the United
States of America. No part of this book may be used or repro-
duced in any manner whatsoever without written permission
except in the case of brief quotations embodied in critical
articles and reviews. For information address HarperCollins
Publishers, 10 East 53rd Street, New York, NY 10022.

FIRST EDITION

Library of Congress Cataloging-in-Publication Data
Peterson, Eugene H.
    Praying with the Early Christians : a year of daily prayers
    and reflections on the words of the early Christians /
    Eugene H. Peterson.—1st ed.
        p.   cm.
    Includes index.
    ISBN 0-06-066517-3
    1. Prayers, Early Christians.   2. Prayer.   3. Devotional
calendars.   I. Title.
BV236.P48   1994
242'.2—dc20   93-45698
                                                                CIP

94 95 96 97 98 99 ❖ BANVA 9 8 7 6 5 4 3 2 1

For
The Earliest Christians
at Christ Our King Presbyterian Church
Bel Air, Maryland

Jean Boyer
Flo Bryant
Barbara Dombroskie
Bill and Barbara Hydro
Eric and Eileen Matthews
Janice Peterson
Mabel Scarborough
Morris and Doris Tibbels

Praying with the Early Christians:
Introduction

CHRISTIANS PRAY. We always have; we always will. We pray because a living God speaks to us and we find ourselves invited into the conversation.

Because the scriptures are a primary witness to God's speaking to us—bringing us into being by his word, shaping salvation in us by his word, blessing us with his word—the scriptures are the basic environment in which we pray. Not the only place, for we also pray while driving our cars, standing in line at the market, taking a shower, and walking on the beach. But still the primary place, for it is in the scriptures that we find ready and dependable access to the words that invite us to pray; it is there that we discover the vocabulary and syntax that are most appropriate in matters of the soul and God.

Holy scripture for Christians is not so much a book we go to for information on God as it is a revealed world in which we are addressed by God and learn to live in response to what we hear. In this God-revealing world we find ourselves in a remarkable conversation, which is to say, in prayer. And we find that we need to cultivate a different kind of reading than we are used to bringing to newspapers and textbooks and computer manuals, reading that is leisurely, repetitive, and reflective. Baron Friedrich von Hügel wrote that it is more like sucking on a lozenge than gulping a meal. It is a way of reading that shapes the heart at the same time that it informs the intellect, sucking out the marrow-nourishment from the bone-words.

But leisurely and repetitively doesn't mean slovenly or lazily. G. K. Chesterton said that there was a great difference between the lively person wanting to read a book and the tired person wanting a book to read.

The necessity for alert and ready responsiveness to the Spirit as we read scripture is on display in a diary entry by Julian Green for October 6, 1941: "The story of the manna gathered and set aside by the Hebrews is deeply significant. It so happened that the manna rotted when it was kept. And perhaps that means that all spiritual reading which is not consumed—by prayer and by works—ends by causing a sort of rotting inside us. You die with a head of fine sayings and a perfectly empty heart."

A little over a quarter of our New Testament scripture was written by St. Luke. His Gospel of Jesus Christ and his Acts of the Apostles are a two-volume work that provides a comprehensive account of the early Christians. My intent in writing these reflections and prayers on St. Luke's masterwork and spreading them over twelve months is to get us modern Christians praying in step with the early Christians, entering into the stories and events and sayings of their lives, being astonished as was the first-century world with their love and witness.

One of the things that always happens as we practice such praying is that our pace slows down. We are no longer in a hurry, calling out to God on the run. We find ourselves lingering in the text, contemplative in the presence of the Spirit and in company with these early Christians. And then we begin to experience the great paradox of prayer: that as we do less, God does more. Energy increases, purpose deepens, zest spills out. Instead of being scattered and distracted, our lives become concentrated in witness and expression, real work in the real world.

I always encourage people who pray to invite others into the praying—in the intentional meeting of friends, in groups gathered for listening and study, in telephoning and letter writing. The early Christians seem to have been most convivial, delighting in one another's company, finding prayer to be as natural in their meetings with one another as conversation and food. In a flat and friendless culture, *Praying with the Early Christians* can bring us deeper both into God and into the human communities without which we cannot live well and whole lives.

Praying with the Early Christians

JANUARY 1

"An Orderly Account"

READ Luke 1:1–4

I too decided, after investigating everything
carefully from the very first, to write an
orderly account for you, most excellent
Theophilus. . . .

Luke 1:3

Luke combines assiduous research and an orderly
mind to create for Theophilus (and us) a clear account of Jesus Christ. The Gospel he writes is
everywhere alive to human interest and brim-
ming with insights regarding God's compassionate salvation.

What do you like best about Luke's Gospel?

PRAYER: Holy Spirit, as you accomplished your
purpose in Luke, the writer of scripture, do the
same in me, the reader of scripture, in the name
of Jesus Christ, my Lord. Amen.

JANUARY 2

"Barren"

READ Luke 1:5–7

> But they had no children, because Elizabeth
> was barren, and both were getting on in
> years.
>
> Luke 1:7

Zechariah and Elizabeth express Judaism previous
to the gospel. They had done everything religion
could do, yet there was an emptiness at the center—their righteousness was admirable, but not
enough: "blameless . . . but barren."

Can you recall another very famous husband
and wife who were childless in their old age?

PRAYER: Dear God, I look at the world (at my own
heart!) and think it's hopeless, no earthly possibility of new life. Then I remember that that is the
very point at which the gospel begins. "In the
deserts of the heart Let the healing fountain start,
In the prison of his days Teach the free man how
to praise" (W. H. Auden, "In Memory of W. B.
Yeats," Collected Poems [New York: Random House,
1976], p. 198). Amen.

"Your Prayer Has Been Heard"

READ Luke 1:8–13

Now at the time of the incense offering,
 the whole assembly of the people was
 praying outside.

Luke 1:10

A multitude of people faithfully gathered at the temple to back Zechariah in prayer. Prayer is the context in which God acts most creatively, the environment in which his promises are announced and his work of salvation begun.

Who are you backing up with your prayers?

PRAYER: O God, as your ministers lead people in prayer in congregations across this land, help me to be a faithful supporter of their leadership, adding my prayers to theirs, and listening to your new word in Jesus Christ. *Amen.*

"Great in the Sight of the Lord"

READ Luke 1:14–17

"You will have joy and gladness, and many
will rejoice at his birth, for he will be
great in the sight of the Lord."

Luke 1:14–15a

The angelic word defines John's task: get people
ready for the Lord. Years later Jesus said of him, "I
tell you, among those born of women no one is
greater than John" (Luke 7:28)—evidence that he
fulfilled the promise made by Gabriel.

What is your favorite phrase in this passage?

PRAYER: Help me, Almighty God, to be alert and
responsive to every word and circumstance you
provide in order to make me ready for you. Turn
my heart to you as you reveal yourself in Christ.
Amen.

JANUARY 5

"How Will I Know . . . ?"

> Zechariah said to the angel, "How will I
> know that this is so? For I am an old man,
> and my wife is getting on in years."
>
> Luke 1:18

It is better to be silent than to weary God with
skeptical questions. We are not responsible for
figuring out how God will fulfill his promise; our
assignment is to wait expectantly in faith and
hope.

Why is God's promise so hard to believe?

PRAYER: God, I seldom understand how you can
fulfill your promises: you promise me so much in
Christ, and you have so little to work with in me.
Forgive me for noisily entertaining doubts when I
could be quietly overflowing with grateful praise.
Amen.

"Greetings, Favored One!"
READ Luke 1:26–31

And he came to her and said, "Greetings,
favored one! The Lord is with you."

Luke 1:28

God's plan is to enter human history in the form
of an infant, born of a woman. The ages of messianic preparation narrow down to one person,
the Virgin Mary, as God makes his choice of a
mother for the Messiah.

What do you suppose were some of Mary's
thoughts?

PRAYER: My heart quickens with gratitude as I
relive Mary's experience, remembering how you
speak similarly to me, causing Christ to be born
anew in my heart. Thank you for new life in
Christ Jesus. *Amen.*

JANUARY 7

"Son of the Most High"
READ Luke 1:32–33

"He will be great, and will be called the
Son of the Most High, and the Lord God
will give to him the throne of his
ancestor David."

Luke 1:32

There is no exaggeration here in the use of super-
latives. Our imaginations are stretched to their
limits to comprehend everything that Jesus will be
to us. And every word is true.

What is your favorite phrase for describing
Jesus?

PRAYER: Almighty God, you have given us your
best in giving your Son, Jesus. Receive my adoration, my gratitude, my praise. Accept my obedience and my worship. Amen.

"Power of the Most High"
READ Luke 1:34–35

> Mary said to the angel, "How can this be,
> since I am a virgin?" The angel said to
> her, "The Holy Spirit will come upon
> you. . . ."
>
> Luke 1:34–35a

To Mary's question (and ours), "How can this be?" the answer is brief and direct: "The Holy Spirit will come upon you." God uses human vessels for his redemptive work, but he uses divine means. Human bodies provide the materials for salvation; the Holy Spirit is the power that makes it happen.

Are you ever doubtful about God's ability to accomplish his will in your life?

PRAYER: "Spirit of God, descend upon my heart; wean it from earth; through all its pulses move; stoop to my weakness, mighty as thou art, and make me love thee as I ought to love" (George Croly, "Spirit of God, Descend Upon My Heart" in The Hymnbook, p. 236). Amen.

"The Servant of the Lord"

READ Luke 1:36–38

> Then Mary said, "Here am I, the servant of
> the Lord; let it be with me according to
> your word."

Luke 1:38a

God has great things to do in us. The question is
never "Can he do it?" but "Will we let him?"
Mary's response, "Let it be with me according to
your word," is the model Christian response.

What is the best way you can respond to God's
word today?

PRAYER: O God, instead of asking questions and
calculating possibilities, I want to be like Mary,
simply to let your word do its work in me, shaping and maturing my spirit to glorify your name.
Amen.

"Blessed Is She Who Believed"

READ Luke 1:39–45

"And blessed is she who believed that there
would be a fulfillment of what was
spoken to her by the Lord."

Luke 1:45

Elizabeth and Mary, one barren and the other a virgin, were both with child by the word of God—contrasting instances of God's ability to create life in the midst of "impossibilities." Their meeting was a sharing of joy: belief results in blessing.

What instance of joy can you share with another today?

PRAYER: Dear Jesus, I don't want to keep the miracle of your life in me secret and hidden—it needs sharing. Lead me to someone with whom I can share the joy of your new life, a kindred spirit whom I can support and strengthen in the faith. *Amen*

"My Soul Magnifies the Lord"

READ Luke 1:46–50

And Mary said,
  "My soul magnifies the Lord,
  and my spirit rejoices in God my
    Savior. . . ."

Luke 1:46–47

Mary's song is purest praise. She realizes and accepts the promises of God intensely and personally. She discovers herself in direct relation to the mighty acts of God.

What is the greatest thing God has done for you?

PRAYER: How grateful I am, O Father, to be part of a community of people who know how to praise, who have so many ways and find so many occasions to express glad gratitude to you. My soul magnifies the Lord! *Amen.*

"He Has Filled the Hungry with Good Things"
READ Luke 1:51–56

". . . he has filled the hungry with good
   things,
and sent the rich away empty."

Luke 1:53

Worldly wisdom says, "them as has, gets." The gospel turns the tables on the world's wisdom. God in Christ reverses the experiences of the worldly wise and instead of exploiting the helpless, saves them.

What needs has God filled in your life?

PRAYER: I am wary of revealing my weaknesses to others, Lord, for fear they will take advantage of me. But I don't have to do that with you—you won't take advantage of me. I confess my emptiness; now fill me with "good things" through Jesus Christ, my Lord. *Amen.*

"His Name Is John"

READ Luke 1:57–66

He asked for a writing tablet and wrote,
"His name is John." And all of them
were amazed.

Luke 1:63

Names reflect expectations. We name our children after people we admire. Everyone thought it would be sufficient that this child follow in his father's footsteps. But God had plans that would take him far beyond family expectations. "John" means "God is gracious."

What does your name mean? Is there any way that it can be made to reflect God's promise in your life?

PRAYER: Gracious God, you have better ideas for me than I ever have for myself. Keep me from thinking meanly or narrowly about who I am. Help me to walk confidently as the new creature you have made of me in Jesus Christ. Amen.

"Looked Favorably . . . and Redeemed"
READ Luke 1:67–75

"Blessed be the Lord God of Israel,
for he has looked favorably on his people
and redeemed them."

Luke 1:68

Zechariah's song is masterful. He sees God's work in all its fullness. God is not remote, far off in the heavens; he comes close and visits his people. And not just to pay a social call—he visits in order to redeem.

What is your favorite Christmas song?

PRAYER: Words can never do justice to the exuberance I feel when I realize what you have done in coming to this earth to redeem me, O God. Your coming releases the deepest springs of praise in my heart. How glad you make me in Jesus! *Amen.*

JANUARY 15

"You Will Go Before the Lord"
READ Luke 1:76–79

"And you, child, will be called the prophet
   of the Most High;
for you will go before the Lord to prepare
   his ways,
to give knowledge of salvation to his
   people
by the forgiveness of their sins."

                       Luke 1:76–77

John's ministry is outlined: he is to prepare the way for the Christ, alerting the populace to his coming so that they will not drift on unawares or be left uninformed regarding the great day.

Are you prepared to celebrate Jesus' birth and accept his presence?

PRAYER: What a lot of help you offer me, God, so that I can give my full attention to your good news in Jesus Christ. Not only Jesus himself as your Word, but also a host of supporting persons (like John) to prepare the way and nurture me in the life of discipleship. Thank you. *Amen.*

"Strong in Spirit"

READ Luke 1:80

The child grew and became strong in
spirit. . . .

Luke 1:80a

The wilderness, away from the distractions and temptations of the city, was the best place for developing the spiritual life. John had, it seems, a long and arduous education to prepare him for his prophetic task.

What does it mean to be "strong in spirit"?

PRAYER: God, I don't want the soft, luxurious ways of the world, but the intense, disciplined ways of the spirit. Lead me to those associations and situations that will put spiritual muscle in me so that I am prepared to serve you well in Jesus Christ. Amen.

JANUARY 17

"Bethlehem"

READ Luke 2:1–5

Joseph also went from the town of
Nazareth in Galilee to Judea, to the city
of David called Bethlehem. . . .

Luke 2:4a

"O little town of Bethlehem, how still we see thee
lie; above thy deep and dreamless sleep the silent
stars go by. Yet in thy dark streets shineth the
everlasting light; the hopes and fears of all the
years are met in thee tonight" (Phillips Brooks,
"O Little Town of Bethlehem").

Compare these verses from Luke with Micah
5:2–4.

PRAYER: I marvel, Almighty God, how you coordinate an emperor's decree, an ancient prophecy, and the coming and going of ordinary people in the insignificant town of Bethlehem to work out your plan of redemption. I praise your wonderful name. Amen.

"Laid Him in a Manger"
READ Luke 2:6–7

And she gave birth to her firstborn son and
wrapped him in bands of cloth, and laid
him in a manger, because there was no
place for them in the inn.

Luke 2:7

The birth of Jesus could not have taken place in
circumstances more modest or rude. He began at
the bottom of the human condition, where people are poor and homeless and rejected, so that he
could raise us all to the heights of salvation.

What difference would it have made if Jesus
had been born in a palace?

PRAYER: "Ah, dearest Jesus, holy Child, make
Thee a bed, soft, undefiled Within my heart, that
it may be A quiet chamber kept for Thee" (Martin
Luther, translated by Catherine Winkworth, "Ah,
Dearest Jesus, Holy Child"). *Amen.*

"Good News of Great Joy"
READ Luke 2:8–12

> But the angel said to them, "Do not be
> afraid; for see—I am bringing you good
> news of great joy for all the people. . . ."
>
> Luke 2:10

The birth of a child brings joy to parents and
friends; the birth of Jesus brings joy to "all the
people," for in this child God reveals his love for
his creation and expresses his power to bring
about every person's salvation.

Among the Christmas cards you received in De-
cember, which one best expresses the birth news
of Jesus Christ for you?

PRAYER: God, you break into the humdrum routines of my life with the best news. My experiences of weariness and hopelessness are suddenly
penetrated by "good news of great joy"—Christ is
born! Amen.

"Glory to God in the Highest Heaven"
READ Luke 2:13–14

"Glory to God in the highest heaven,
and on earth peace among those whom he
favors!"

Luke 2:14

The birth of Christ makes a connection between what happens in heaven ("glory to God in the highest heaven") and what happens on earth ("on earth peace"). The two realms of heaven and earth, separated by our sin, are rejoined in this new life in which God shares his presence.

What experience of peace have you had that seems to result from Jesus' birth?

PRAYER: All praise to you, O God. What happy songs fill the air these days! Your coming in Jesus has created the will to sing and praise all over the land. I add my voice to the music of multitudes in heaven and earth. Hallelujah! *Amen.*

"Let Us Go Now to Bethlehem"
READ Luke 2:15–18

> So they went with haste and found Mary
> and Joseph, and the child lying in the
> manger.
>
> Luke 2:16

The shepherds were the first witnesses. Not content just to hear the angelic choir and rejoice in the good news, they became participants verifying the birth of Christ with their own eyes and then spreading the proclamation.

Are you as eager as the shepherds to share what you know about Jesus?

PRAYER: Everyone has an opinion on religion, Lord, but not many people are thinking about Christ. Help me to keep my eye on the center, on Jesus, and share what I see with any others who are distracted from faith. *Amen.*

"Pondered Them in Her Heart"

READ Luke 2:19

But Mary treasured all these words and
pondered them in her heart.

Luke 2:19

Meditation is a nearly lost art—and not easy to acquire in a noisy world. Mary, quietly and meditatively, brooded over the wondrous events surrounding her infant son, letting their significance sink deeply into her spirit.

Do you have a regular time for silent meditation before God?

PRAYER: God, let me withdraw for a while now from the chatter and gossip of the world, and let your words sink deeply into my mind and spirit. In the quietness of these moments help me to realize the eternal significance of the birth of Jesus, in whose name I pray. *Amen.*

"Glorifying and Praising God"

READ Luke 2:20

The shepherds returned, glorifying and
praising God for all they had heard and
seen, as it had been told them.

Luke 2:20

"Nothing was ever praised enough," said G. K.
Chesterton. Since God has invaded the world in
Jesus, everyone is seen to be a target for his saving
love. No wonder the shepherds were exuberant.

How can you express your praise for Christ's
birth today?

PRAYER: What a flood of joy you pour over my
life, O God. You have convinced me that you love
me, persuaded me that you will save me, assured
me of eternal life with you—all through Jesus
Christ my Lord through whom I offer praise.
Amen.

"He Was Called Jesus"

READ Luke 2:21

After eight days had passed, it was time to
circumcise the child; and he was called
Jesus, the name given by the angel
before he was conceived in the womb.

Luke 2:21

Jesus is the name above every name. It means
"God saves." No other name brings such sure
hope for salvation. His birth is the occasion for realizing that God has entered into our own personal existence to do his saving work.

Compare this verse with Matthew 1:21–25.

PRAYER: "O holy Child of Bethlehem, Descend
to us, we pray; cast out our sin, and enter in, Be
born in us today. We hear the Christmas angels
The great glad tidings tell; O come to us, abide
with us, Our Lord Emmanuel" (Phillips Brooks,
"O Little Town of Bethlehem"). *Amen.*

JANUARY 25

"Holy to the Lord"
READ Luke 2:22–24

. . (as it is written in the law of the Lord,
  "Every firstborn male shall be designated
  as holy to the Lord"). . . .

Luke 2:23

Jesus is the fulfillment of the "hopes and fears of all the years," not the repudiation of them. The offering in the temple signifies that. He is the completion in which we see that God's hand works in all things to bring about salvation.

How will you express your worship to God today?

PRAYER: "Yea, Lord, we greet Thee, born this happy morning; O Jesus, to Thee be all glory given; Word of the Father, Now in flesh appearing! O come, let us adore Him, Christ, the Lord!" (Translated by Frederick Oakley, "O Come, All Ye Faithful," in *The Hymnbook*, p. 170). *Amen.*

JANUARY 26

"Simeon"
READ Luke 2:25–26

Now there was a man in Jerusalem whose
name was Simeon; this man was
righteous and devout, looking forward
to the consolation of Israel, and the Holy
Spirit rested on him.

Luke 2:25

Simeon brought to the birth of Christ the deter-
mination of the psalmist who wrote: "I wait for
the Lord, my soul waits, and in his word I hope"
(Psalm 130:5). Many centuries of longing were
concentrated in the old man. No expectation that
is rooted in the promises of God is disappointed.

What hopes do you have that find their focus in
Jesus?

PRAYER: God, my imagination is crisscrossed with
whims and wishes—most of them are doomed to
disappointment. But there are deeper desires in
me, implanted by your Holy Spirit, that are fulfilled in Jesus Christ. Thank you for making good
on those promises in Jesus. *Amen.*

"Dismissing Your Servant in Peace"
READ Luke 2:27–32

> "Master, now you are dismissing your
>   servant in peace,
> according to your word. . . ."

Luke 2:29

The song of Simeon displays the wise contentment of a long life lived in devotion to God. Simeon is prepared to die peacefully, not because of the great things he has accomplished that he can view with pride, but because he has seen God accomplish his purpose.

What would you like to see before you die?

PRAYER: Help me so to live, O God, that when I approach the time of my death I may look back with neither regret nor panic, but rather with quiet gratitude for all I have seen and experienced of your grace through Jesus Christ. Amen.

"Amazed"

And the child's father and mother were
amazed at what was being said about him.

Luke 2:33

God's wondrous plan of salvation, shaped in the form of Jesus, is beyond human calculation. Paul expressed what Mary and Joseph experienced: "O the depth of the riches and wisdom and knowledge of God! How unsearchable are his judgments and how inscrutable his ways!" (Romans 11:33).

What aspect of Jesus' birth seems most wonderful to you?

PRAYER: "Christ, by highest heaven adored; Christ, the Everlasting Lord! Late in time behold Him come To the earth from heaven's home; veiled in flesh the Godhead see; hail th' incarnate Deity, Pleased as man with men to dwell, Jesus our Emmanuel . . . glory to the newborn King" (Charles Wesley, "Hark, the Herald Angels Sing"). Amen.

JANUARY 29

"A Sign That Will Be Opposed"
READ Luke 2:34–35

Then Simeon blessed them and said to his
mother Mary, "This child is destined for
the falling and the rising of many in
Israel, and to be a sign that will be
opposed. . . ."

Luke 2:34

A dark strain of suffering is sounded even while
the glad angelic choirs hymn jubilation. The joy
of Christ's coming is deep enough to absorb the
pain that comes with rejection, and powerful
enough to deal with the sin that will result in
crucifixion.

What was the "sword" that would pierce Mary's
heart?

PRAYER: I know, O God, that the joy you bring is
not the kind that avoids suffering or sidesteps evil.
You confront sin, deal with it, suffer because of it,
and out of it all fashion a redemption for the
world. For this I thank you, in Jesus' name. Amen.

"Anna"

READ Luke 2:36–38

There was also a prophet, Anna the
daughter of Phanuel, of the tribe of
Asher.

Luke 2:36a

The temple in Jesus' day, like the church in ours, was full of those who had their minds on business and gossip. But Anna was there to worship. Her single-mindedness was rewarded when she recognized Jesus as God's redemption.

What do you go to church for?

PRAYER: God, keep me from frivolous or selfish concerns when I go to church. Help me to give myself to listening to your word to me, and giving thanks for your presence there in Jesus Christ, in whose strong name I pray. *Amen.*

"The Child Grew"
READ Luke 2:39–40

> The child grew and became strong, filled
> with wisdom; and the favor of God was
> upon him.
>
> Luke 2:40

Scripture is silent about Jesus' childhood. We do,
though, know the results of those years of growth:
Jesus developed in body ("became strong"), in
mind ("filled with wisdom"), and in spirit ("the
favor of God was upon him")—a balanced, complete growth that would produce, in maturity, the
"new Adam."

What are your "growth" goals as a Christian?

PRAYER: Help me, O Father, to grow up into
Christ after the pattern he set for me, treating my
body with respect so that it can be strong in your
service, developing my mind so that it can be wise
in your ways, but most of all responding to your
grace in Christ so that I may experience your favor
in all I do. Amen.

"Prepare the Way of the Lord"

READ Luke 3:1–6

"The voice of one crying out in the
    wilderness:
'Prepare the way of the Lord,
make his paths straight.'"

Luke 3:4b

Centuries of messianic anticipation, nurtured by prophets like Isaiah, were brought to a climax by John the Baptist. His rigorous preaching purged the public mind of cant and prepared a people for their Savior.

Who has been important in preparing you to respond to Christ?

PRAYER: Make the old prophetic words sound fresh and alive in my ears, O God, so that I will be expectant and ready, alert for the gospel work you will do in me today. *Amen.*

"You Brood of Vipers!"

READ Luke 3:7–9

John said to the crowds that came out to be
baptized by him, "You brood of vipers!
Who warned you to flee from the wrath
to come?"

Luke 3:7

John prepared the people for God's judgment by
ripping off their thin veneer of respectability and
showing them what was wrong in their hearts.
Realization of judgment is preparation for receiving forgiveness in Jesus Christ.

What do you think the Pharisees expected from
baptism?

PRAYER: Dear God, I know that you see through
every pretense I fabricate, penetrate every hypocrisy, and know me for what I am. Through the
severity of your judgment help me to realize the
mercy of your forgiveness and be made new in
Jesus. Amen.

FEBRUARY 3

"What Then Should We Do?"
READ Luke 3:10–14

> And the crowds asked him, "What then
> should we do?"
>
> Luke 3:10

Repentance marks that moment of insight when we realize that, whether through rebellion or wandering, we have missed God's way and then are willing to be directed to it. Repentance is not an emotion nearly so much as it is an ethical decision. It is not a wallowing in futile regrets; it is a plunge into faith.

Which of the three groups questioning John is closest to your life situation?

PRAYER: What shall I do, Lord? What specific things can I do this day that will put your will into action in my life? How can I express in my work and among my friends the new life in Christ? *Amen.*

"His Winnowing Fork"

READ Luke 3:15–17

"His winnowing fork is in his hand, to
clear his threshing floor and to gather
the wheat into his granary; but the chaff
he will burn with unquenchable fire."

Luke 3:17

John's prophetic task is not to make people feel
good by flattering or entertaining them. Nor is he
a religious journalist with the latest information
about God. He presents the majestic reality of God
in the person of the Christ, to whom we must
respond.

Compare this reference to chaff with that in
Psalm 1.

PRAYER: Father, help me to pick out from the
noises of the crowd the voices of your prophets
who give clear, bold, and authentic witness to
you; and after I have heard them, move me to respond in obedience to everything you have for me
in Jesus Christ, in whose name I pray. Amen.

"Herod the Ruler"
READ Luke 3:18–20

But Herod the ruler, who had been
rebuked by him because of Herodias, his
brother's wife, and because of all the evil
things that Herod had done, added to
them all by shutting up John in prison.
Luke 3:19–20

Herod, fascinated by John, was also irritated by
him, for the truth John preached interfered with
the ruler's personal affairs. Herod valued personal
comfort more than truth and so, in an attempt to
silence God's word, he put the preacher in prison.
It was a blustering charade of strength that masked
the weakest thing he ever did.

Have you ever tried to avoid facing the truth?

PRAYER: I don't always like what you say to me,
God. Quite frankly, life would go more smoothly
without some of your words. You raise issues I
would just as soon avoid. You confront me with
realities I would rather ignore. In addition to your
prophetic word, give me a spirit of courage to
face your truth and accept your total lordship over
my life, in Jesus Christ. Amen.

"Well Pleased"

READ Luke 3:21–22

And a voice came from heaven, "You are
my Son, the Beloved; with you I am well
pleased."

Luke 3:22b

In Jesus' baptism God demonstrated his pleasure
in the great act of salvation that entered our history in the Christ. This way of salvation is no
grudging fulfillment of divine duty but a delightful outpouring of the Spirit on the Son to do the
work of the Father.

What does the dove symbolize?

PRAYER. How wonderful, O God, to be part of
such a glad exchange of sounds and acts. What
you said to Jesus, I hear you saying to me. As you
announce your good pleasure in my salvation, I
will live in daily joy. *Amen.*

"He Began His Work"
READ Luke 3:23–38

Jesus was about thirty years old when he
began his work.

Luke 3:23a

Jesus Christ begins something new; he also completes something very old, something that stretches
all the way back to Adam. He is the point where
God starts all over again with his ancient people
and "makes all things new." But none of our past
is lost or discarded in the new creation that is
fashioned by Christ's ministry.

Why do you think Luke included this long list
of names?

PRAYER: Begin something in me, O God—a life
fresh with love and grace, a life in which Jesus
Christ lives in me "new every morning" (Lamentations 3:23). *Amen.*

FEBRUARY 8

"Wilderness"

READ Luke 4:1–13

Jesus, full of the Holy Spirit, returned from
the Jordan and was led by the Spirit in
the wilderness, where for forty days he
was tempted by the devil. He ate
nothing at all during those days, and
when they were over, he was famished.

Luke 4:1–2

At the Jordan Jesus experienced the best that God
could bestow on him; in the wilderness he endured the worst that Satan could inflict on him.
Satan's testings probed into the extremities of existence; the results showed that Jesus is gloriously
competent to be our Savior.

Which of the three temptations are you most
likely to face?

PRAYER: I come with confidence to you, Lord, in
my troubles, knowing "we do not have a high
priest who is unable to sympathize with our
weaknesses, but . . . one who in every respect has
been tested as we are" (Hebrews 4:15). Guide
and sustain me in my times of temptation. *Amen.*

FEBRUARY 9

"The Year of the Lord's Favor"
READ Luke 4:14–21

"He has sent me to proclaim release to the
captives
and recovery of sight to the blind,
to let the oppressed go free,
to proclaim the year of the Lord's favor."

Luke 4:18b–19

All time and scripture come to climax and fulfillment in Jesus' ministry. Old promises, redolent
with hope but dusty with age, come alive and
sparkle in his presence. Jesus' one-sentence synagogue sermon does everything a sermon needs to
do—it announces the completion of God's salvation and it applies it to the present.

How many different actions are described in
the Isaiah passage?

PRAYER: Enter my history, Lord Jesus. Invade my
life with your rule. Complete your work in my
heart. Be my guide as I explore your kingdom and
participate in its marvels. *Amen.*

"Is Not This Joseph's Son?"

READ Luke 4:22–30

All spoke well of him and were amazed at
the gracious words that came from his
mouth. They said, "Is not this Joseph's
son?"

Luke 4:22

Some people's philosophy is, "If I have to be a
molehill, I will make sure there aren't any mountains." Men attempted this with Jesus, trying to
trim him down to a size they were comfortable
with (i.e., Joseph's son). And when he wouldn't be
reduced to their level, they angrily rejected him.

What was the significance of Jesus' references
to the widow and the Syrian?

PRAYER: I wonder how many times my unbelief
has prevented your mighty works in my life, Jesus.
Save me from the small-minded attitudes that
screen out everything magnificent and glorious.
Amen.

"He Spoke with Authority"
READ Luke 4:31–37

They were astounded at his teaching,
  because he spoke with authority.

Luke 4:32

The synagogue had, through the years, become a place where men exchanged pious opinions; in Jesus it became the place where God's word was authoritatively proclaimed and his deliverance demonstrated.

How did the people know Jesus had authority?

PRAYER: O God, surprise me as you surprised those people in Capernaum. The next time I go to church expecting nothing more than some friendly, religious talk with my friends, invade my complacent piety with your commanding word in Christ. *Amen.*

"Simon's House"

READ Luke 4:38–39

After leaving the synagogue he entered
Simon's house. Now Simon's mother-in-
law was suffering from a high fever, and
they asked him about her.

Luke 4:38

Jesus demonstrated his redemptive rule in the
public places of worship (the synagogue) but also
in the private places of family life. There it is significant that the act of healing results immediately
in an act of service: "she . . . began to serve them"
(v. 39).

For what has God's salvation given you
strength?

PRAYER: The intense, intimate existence that takes
place within the four walls of my house needs
your lordship, Jesus. There is nearly always someone who is ailing, either in body or in spirit. Heal,
Lord, and equip us to serve one another. Amen.

FEBRUARY 13

"Into a Deserted Place"
READ Luke 4:40–44

At daybreak he departed and went into a
deserted place. And the crowds were
looking for him; and when they reached
him, they wanted to prevent him from
leaving them.

Luke 4:42

Jesus rhythmically alternated between the crowds
and solitude. In the "deserted place" his body and
spirit, fatigued by the intensities of ministry, were,
in prayer, restored and equipped to move back
into the stream of healing and preaching.

What provision do you make for prayer in your
schedule?

PRAYER: Help me to achieve that easy, rhythmic
movement that seemed such a natural part of your
life, Jesus, moving back and forth from giving
myself to others in service to giving myself to you
in prayer. *Amen.*

FEBRUARY 14

"Beside the Lake"

READ Luke 5:1–11

. . he saw two boats there at the shore of
the lake; the fishermen had gone out of
them and were washing their nets.

Luke 5:2

Jesus invaded the workaday world where men
were busy at their jobs. The lake of Gennesaret
was the industrial fishing center of northern
Galilee. The gospel is not only for places of worship and the gatherings of family—it also centers
the Monday-through-Friday world of work.

How does being a Christian make a difference
in your work?

PRAYER: Lord, take my working skills, the things I
am good at in my job, and put them to the uses of
discipleship. Let me hear your call within the routines of my daily round, and let me respond as
quickly as did Simon, James, and John. Amen.

"Touched Him"

READ Luke 5:12–16

Then Jesus stretched out his hand, touched
him, and said, "I do choose. Be made
clean." Immediately the leprosy left him.

Luke 5:13

Lepers in the first century were untouchable.
Powerful taboos surrounded their existence. But
Jesus was not restricted by customs or traditions.
Not what human beings habitually thought, but
what God eternally willed, provided the direction
for his ministry.

Who are some "untouchable" people in your
existence?

PRAYER: Why do I suppose, God, that you are unwilling or unable to work your will among certain people or classes of people? Why am I always
making exceptions to your compassion? You have
never yet been limited by human precedents. You
are always doing something new. Praise your
name! Amen.

"Your Sins Are Forgiven You"

READ Luke 5:17–26

When he saw their faith, he said, "Friend,
your sins are forgiven you."

Luke 5:20

We think we know what we need and go to great
lengths to get it. Jesus, though, penetrates beneath our surface symptoms and deals with us at
the deepest level of all: he forgives our sins.

What do you think you need from God?

PRAYER: A lot of people have ideas on how I can
improve my life. How grateful I am that you,
Jesus, go far beyond "improvements" and "good
advice." You go to the center of my need, forgiv
ing my sins and setting me free to be the person
you created in love and joy. *Amen.*

"Sinners"

READ Luke 5:27–32

> The Pharisees and their scribes were
> complaining to his disciples, saying,
> "Why do you eat and drink with tax
> collectors and sinners?"
>
> Luke 5:30

The error persists: despite very clear evidence to the contrary, men and women insist on thinking of Christians as the good people whom God likes. But Jesus said that Christians are the bad people whom God calls to salvation. The church, like a hospital, is full of sick people in the process of being healed, not well people displaying their prowess.

Do you ever criticize the church for being hospitable to not-very-nice people?

PRAYER: Lord, if I were self-sufficient and satisfied with my life I wouldn't bother you—even with this prayer. But I am not adequate. I need your healing in my body and soul. I accept you as my "great Physician," O Christ. *Amen.*

"Fresh Wineskins"

READ Luke 5:33–39

"But new wine must be put into fresh
   wineskins."

Luke 5:38

Rigid religious customs cannot carry the explosive joy of the gospel. The presence of Christ in our lives demands expression in joyous celebration and loving generosity.

What are some "old wineskins" you need to discard?

PRAYER: Lord, save me from gloomy traditions and stiff precedents. Help me to find new, fresh ways of letting the world know that because you are alive in my heart, a celebration is going on. Amen.

"Lord of the Sabbath"

READ Luke 6:1–5

Then he said to them, "The Son of Man is
lord of the sabbath."

Luke 6:5

Sin takes even the best of things (sabbath obser-
vance, for instance) and turns it upside down,
making a burden out of what was created as a
blessing. Jesus, though, marvelously puts everything right side up again, and we are free to praise
God in love rather than keep rules in fear.

How do you observe the sabbath?

PRAYER: How wonderful to find that the world is
a creation for me to live in and enjoy, and not a
probation to be endured. Your presence, Jesus,
makes it joyous and free. Amen.

"To Save Life or to Destroy It?"
READ Luke 6:6–11

Then Jesus said to them, "I ask you, is it
lawful to do good or to do harm on the
sabbath, to save life or to destroy it?"

Luke 6:9

Jesus forces a clarification of motives: Do we really want to help and heal? Or are we mostly interested in getting our own way and getting rid of
anyone (even God) who obstructs us?

Who were the Pharisees?

PRAYER: Be quick, O God, to expose those little
stratagems and excuses that I use to avoid your
life giving ministry, excuses like "It isn't the right
day" and "It was never done this way." Amen.

FEBRUARY 21

"Whom He Also Named Apostles"
READ Luke 6:12–16

And when day came, he called his disciples
and chose twelve of them, whom he
also named apostles. . . .

Luke 6:13

Apostle means "a sent person"—in this case, one
who is sent by Christ to repeat his words and
continue his works. The call and training of the
twelve by Jesus initiated a strategy that continues
into the present, as the Holy Spirit gives each
Christian the gifts to represent Christ in the world.

What has God sent you to do?

PRAYER: I want to move from those multitudes
who pressed to get a look at you, Jesus, to the
company of disciples who are with you. I do not
want only to receive your blessings; I want to
share your work. *Amen.*

"Blessed Are You . . . Woe to You"
READ Luke 6:17–26

Then he looked up at his disciples and said:
"Blessed are you who are poor,
    for yours is the kingdom of God."

Luke 6:20

Four conditions that human beings ordinarily assume to be hopeless and undesirable are shown by Jesus to be the very places where God begins his best work. And four conditions that are supposed to free us from all worry are shown to be the most perilous of states when God is not at their center.

Which of the eight conditions best describes your life right now?

PRAYER: Bless me, dear God. Come to me in my needs and difficulties—the things I am used to calling my problems—and show me how they are where you are, making me a whole person, saved in and through Jesus Christ. Amen.

"Love Your Enemies"
READ Luke 6:27–31

"But I say to you that listen, Love your
enemies, do good to those who hate
you. . . ."

Luke 6:27

Lives that are rooted in God's act of love for us
in Christ—"while we still were sinners" (Romans
5:8)—are capable of reproducing it among others.
But without that base, the command to "love your
enemies" is little more than a pious platitude.

Compare this with Romans 5:6–11.

PRAYER: Lord, here are the people toward whom I
feel enmity: . . . [name them]. Now, help me to
make the first move toward them in love, no
longer permitting my feelings about them or their
feelings about me to dominate our lives, but letting your command and your example show us
how to live with one another. *Amen.*

"Be Merciful"

READ Luke 6:32–38

"Be merciful, just as your Father is merciful."

Luke 6:36

The relationship between ungrateful and selfish people (like ourselves) and a kind and merciful God is disclosed in Jesus Christ. It is in observing that relationship, rather than by calculating the fine points of justice or brooding over "my rights," that the Christian learns how to treat difficult people.

Who is one ungrateful person you find it difficult to deal with?

PRAYER: Father, is your mercy never ending? Does your patience never run out? Do you never tire of my selfishness and ingratitude? Incredibly, the answer seems to be no. The least I can do, then, is to pass some of it on; help me to be merciful to others even as you are merciful to me. *Amen.*

FEBRUARY 25

"The Log in Your Own Eye"
READ Luke 6:39–45

"Why do you see the speck in your
neighbor's eye, but do not notice the log
in your own eye?"

Luke 6:41

Jesus, with engaging humor and penetrating seriousness, pillories all who substitute moral talk
for being moral. Dickens created an example in
Pecksniff: ". . . a most exemplary man, fuller of
virtuous precept than a copy-book. Some people
likened him to a direction-post, which is always
telling the way to a place and never goes there"
(Charles Dickens, *Martin Chuzzlewit*).

What moral act would you rather talk about
than engage in?

PRAYER: When I, O God, start advising others on
what I am supposed to be doing myself and talking about others' faults when I should be confess-
ing my own, interrupt my folly and expose my
hypocrisy, in the name of and for the sake of Jesus
Christ. *Amen.*

FEBRUARY 26

"Foundation on Rock"
READ Luke 6:46–49

"That one is like a man building a house,
who dug deeply and laid the foundation
on rock; when a flood arose, the river
burst against that house but could not
shake it, because it had been well built."

Luke 6:48

Jesus' words are not polished sayings displayed
for our admiration; nor are they textbook arguments provided for intellectual stimulation. They
are practical, foundational realities upon which
we build our everyday lives.

Pick out one sentence from Luke 6 that you will
use as a foundation rock in your meditation today.

PRAYER: Thank you, God, for solid, unshakable
words upon which I can confidently build my life.
"How firm a foundation!" All praise to you, my
Rock and my Salvation. Amen.

"Only Speak the Word"

READ Luke 7:1–10

". . . therefore I did not presume to come
to you. But only speak the word, and let
my servant be healed."

Luke 7:7

The centurion is memorable for a number of qualities: his generosity, his humility, his compassion. Most remarkable, though, is his faith—his readiness to let his deepest concerns be ordered and controlled by the word of God.

What are your deepest concerns?

PRAYER: Say the word, only, O God; "I ask no dream, no prophet ecstasies, no sudden rending of the veil of clay, no angel visitant, no opening skies; but take the dimness of my soul away" (George Croly, "Spirit of God, Descend Upon My Heart" in *The Hymnbook*, p. 236). *Amen.*

"Favorably on His People"
READ Luke 7:11–17

Fear seized all of them; and they glorified
God, saying, "A great prophet has risen
among us!" and "God has looked
favorably on his people!"

Luke 7:16

Zechariah, in his great hymn, twice used the verb
"visited" in prophetic anticipation of what God
was about to do (Luke 7:16, RSV). Here is the
verb again, not this time, though, in anticipation
but in description of the actual visitation: a story
of what happens when God visits his people.

Why were the people afraid?

PRAYER: Sometimes, Father, I feel overcome by
the world's distress—tragedies in the lives of
friends, pain in the bodies of millions. So much
sadness! So much suffering! It is then that I need
your visitation so that there is more to my inner
life than "weeping with those who weep." I need
a visitation that breaks into the funeral procession
of the world and makes a parade of resurrection-
praise out of it. Amen.

"Go and Tell John"

READ Luke 7:18–23

And he answered them, "Are you the one
who is to come, or are we to wait for
another?"

Luke 7:19

Is Jesus all there is, or do we need to look for a
supplement? John's question is still being asked.
And the answer is as convincing as ever: Jesus
does everything for humanity that needs to be
done—all are made whole in their relationship
with him.

Why do you think John was in doubt?

PRAYER: How magnificent your salvation, Lord.
How complete your work among your people.
You deal with each of us according to our need,
making us whole for love and glory. Thank you.
Amen.

"The People of This Generation"
READ Luke 7:24–35

"To what then will I compare the people of
this generation, and what are they like?"

Luke 7:31

Capricious and inconstant, some people shop for
religion the same way they shop for a pair of
shoes, rejecting this for being too austere, then, at
another time, that for being too casual. They do
not have reasons—only moods and whims.

Do you allow your moods to overinfluence
your faith?

PRAYER: "I bind my heart this tide to the Galilean's
side, to the wounds of Calvary, to the Christ who
died for me. I bind my soul this day to the brother
far away, and the brother near at hand, in this
town, and in this land" (Lauchlan MacLean Watt,
"I Bind My Heart This Tide"). Amen.

"Shown Great Love"

READ Luke 7:36–50

"Therefore, I tell you, her sins, which were
many, have been forgiven; hence she has
shown great love. But the one to whom
little is forgiven, loves little."

Luke 7:47

A Pharisee, Simon, had invited Jesus to dinner to
engage in dispassionate moral discourse, and was
irritated at the emotional intrusion of an immoral
woman. But the woman had found in Jesus a for-
giving Savior; overwhelmed with gratitude, she
expressed herself in sacrificial love.

Do you think you would have been critical of
the woman?

PRAYER: "Master, no offering Costly and sweet, May
we, like Magdalene, Lay at Thy feet; Yet may love's
incense rise, Sweeter than sacrifice, Dear Lord, to
Thee, Dear Lord, to Thee" (Edwin P. Parker, "Master, No Offering Costly and Sweet"). Amen.

"Some Women Who Had Been Cured"
READ Luke 8:1–3

. . . as well as some women who had been
cured of evil spirits and infirmities. . . .

Luke 8:2a

Luke, more than the other Gospel writers, gives us
details about women: they have names—their
identity is recognized and respected; and they
have means—their gifts of ministry are accepted
as significant. In the presence of Jesus, both who
we are and what we have are important.

What gifts of yours are valuable in Christ's ministry?

PRAYER: Lord Jesus, I resent it when I am lumped
in a crowd or labeled under a category; and I
appreciate it when I am called by my own name,
and allowed to offer my gifts for important
work—especially when it is you who calls my
name and your work in which I share. *Amen.*

MARCH 5

"Ears to Hear"
READ Luke 8:4–15

As he said this, he called out, "Let anyone
with ears to hear listen!"

Luke 8:8b

Are we good listeners? Or are we so busy chatter-
ing that we never let our Lord's words take deep
root in us? The four soils are four ways to listen to
God's word.

What kind of soil are you?

PRAYER: You speak your seed words of love and
salvation in scripture and sermon, O God. Yet so
many of them never take root. Forgive me. Give
me a listening ear so that I will bear a good harvest for you. *Amen.*

"Nothing Is Hidden"

READ Luke 8:16–18

> "For nothing is hidden that will not be
> disclosed, nor is anything secret that will
> not become known and come to light."
>
> Luke 8:17

The whole fun in having secrets is in telling them
to others. The gospel is not something to ponder
privately; it is to be proclaimed joyously in public.
The secret? God in Christ is in the world, loving
and redeeming us

What secret do you have to share?

PRAYER: Help me to be generous with all I have
received from you, O Christ, not hoarding your
love, not hiding your gifts, but telling your secret
and sharing your riches. *Amen.*

"My Mother and My Brothers"

READ Luke 8:19–21

But he said to them, "My mother and my brothers are those who hear the word of God and do it."

Luke 8:21

Christ established a new family in which we find the intimacies of love, not in the circumstances of blood ties but in the deeper loyalties of doing God's will. God's will reaches deeper into our lives than do the roots of family trees.

Who are some "mothers" and "brothers" God has given to you?

PRAYER: Dear God, lead me ever deeper into the community of people who are doing your will. Teach me how to live with and enjoy the expanded family that you provide in this Christian way. *Amen.*

"There Was a Calm"
READ Luke 8:22–25

They went to him and woke him up,
  shouting, "Master, Master, we are
  perishing!" And he woke up and
  rebuked the wind and the raging waves;
  they ceased, and there was a calm.

Luke 8:24

The world is full of things that frighten us. It is not remarkable that we cry out to God, "We are perishing!" Christ's response, though, is remarkable: he cares; he "wills not the death of a sinner"; his word restores peace to our lives.

What are you frightened of?

PRAYER: I get upset, Lord, over every storm, thinking the ship is going down. I forget that it is your ship—that you made this world and are perfectly capable of taking care of it. Keep me today from underestimating the power of your peace. Amen.

"Legion"

READ Luke 8:26–33

> Jesus then asked him, "What is your
> name?" He said, "Legion"; for many
> demons had entered him.

Luke 8:30

Sin splinters us into a thousand conflicting desires that riot within us. Christ's lordship expels the demonic mob and restores a single, gracious rule.
What conflicts are you aware of in your life?

PRAYER: "Give me an undivided heart to revere your name" (Psalm 86:11). I need your lordship, O Christ; rule over the competing passions and unruly ambitions of my spirit. *Amen.*

"Return to Your Home"

READ Luke 8:34–39

> "Return to your home, and declare how
> much God has done for you." So he
> went away, proclaiming throughout the
> city how much Jesus had done for him.
>
> Luke 8:39

A depth experience with Christ makes us want to stay around and continue the ecstasy. But he won't permit it—he sends us to work. He wants us to do more than enjoy our conversion; he wants us to share it with others.

Why were the Gerasenes fearful?

PRAYER: Forgive me, Lord, for the times I have taken your gifts but not used them. Help me this day to take your new life into the areas where my personal relationships are thickest: the kitchen, the bedroom, the workplace, the supermarket. *Amen.*

MARCH 11

"No One Could Cure Her"
READ Luke 8:40–48

Now there was a woman who had been
suffering from hemorrhages for twelve
years; and though she had spent all she
had on physicians, no one could cure her.
Luke 8:43

Search for help produces an unbelievable quantity
of frustration and disappointment. We reach out
in desperation and get, for our trouble, empty promises. Until we touch Christ—and then healing is
complete.

What, in your life, needs healing?

PRAYER: "The healing of His seamless dress Is by our
beds of pain; We touch Him in life's throng and
press, And we are whole again" (John Greenleaf
Whittier, "Immortal Love, Forever Full"). Blessed be
your name, O God. *Amen.*

"Get Up!"

READ Luke 8:49–56

> But he took her by the hand and called out,
>   "Child, get up!"
>
> Luke 8:54

The "get up" theme is embedded deeply in the gospel story. It comes to a climax in our Lord's resurrection. The raising of the little girl is proof that a word of Christ has power to bring us to life.

How do you account for the command to secrecy in verse 56?

PRAYER: Lord, you don't just put on bandages or hand out aspirin; you reach down to the deepest levels of my need and raise me up. What a savior! Amen.

"He Sent Them Out"

READ Luke 9:1–6

> . . . and he sent them out to proclaim the
> kingdom of God and to heal.
>
> Luke 9:2

Commanded to travel light and to be indifferent to people's opinions, the disciples are focused on repeating the works of Christ after him. Mature Christians do not huddle together for warmth around the love of Christ; they venture into strange and even hostile places to represent that love to others.

What authority do you have as a disciple of Christ?

PRAYER: Do you really have that much confidence in me, Lord? Are you sure you want to trust me with a ministry that is so weighty? I submit myself to your guidance as I seek to be obedient to your commands, sharing your words and ministries with others. *Amen.*

MARCH 14

"He Tried to See Him"
READ Luke 9:7–9

Herod said, "John I beheaded; but who is
  this about whom I hear such things?"
And he tried to see him.

Luke 9:9

Herod is endlessly curious, but his curiosity never
leads to commitment. He was fascinated with
John until that man's presence became inconve-
nient—and then he had him killed. Now he is interested in Jesus. Will this interest change Herod's
life? There is no evidence for it. Hobbies, even
when they are religious hobbies, are only diversions.

Do you ever mistake curiosity about Christ for
commitment to him?

PRAYER: Lord Jesus, it is easy for me to assume
that, when I am interested in spiritual things and
talking about God, I am on the right track. Show
me that I am not on the right track until I am actually walking on it. Amen.

"You Give Them Something to Eat"
READ Luke 9:10–17

> But he said to them, "You give them
> something to eat." They said, "We have
> no more than five loaves and two fish—
> unless we are to go and buy food for all
> these people."
>
> Luke 9:13

Our gifts are just a starting place for God. Our inadequate offerings become, through the power of the Holy Spirit, an abundant feast for many. The life we share with others does not consist of the impressiveness of our gifts but of Christ's action in our gifts.

What gifts will you offer to Christ?

PRAYER: Lord, what will you do with my gift today? In itself it isn't much, but you have never yet been limited by my poverty. Take what I have, bless and break, and give to someone in need. *Amen.*

"Who Do You Say That I Am?"
READ Luke 9:18–22

> He said to them, "But who do you say that
> I am?" Peter answered, "The Messiah of
> God."
>
> Luke 9:20

Each of us has to make a personal decision about Jesus. Out of several alternatives we must, like the disciples, make up our own minds. To decide that he is "Christ" is to accept him as the one God has chosen to be the way of our salvation.

Who do you say that he is?

PRAYER: Let me, Jesus, say the name "Christ" with a renewed sense of its pivotal power: that on you is centered all the work of God for my salvation; that I need to turn to no other; that you are worthy to receive all my adoration. *Amen.*

"If Any Want"

READ Luke 9:23–27

> Then he said to them all, "If any want to
> become my followers, let them deny
> themselves and take up their cross daily
> and follow me."
>
> Luke 9:23

Jesus confronts us with a crossroads decision: to live for self, indulging the whims and desires of pride, or to live for Christ, following his commands and purpose.

What, in you, needs to be denied?

PRAYER: It is not easy, Lord, to relinquish my way and choose yours. I am a bundle of selfish demands and aspirations. Give me the grace to set them behind me and make the choices that proclaim your lordship. You've been over this road before and know it better than I ever will; I want to follow you. *Amen.*

"My Son, My Chosen"
READ Luke 9:28–36

Then from the cloud came a voice that
said, "This is my Son, my Chosen; listen
to him!"

Luke 9:35

God endorses Jesus as Son and Messiah at the
miracle of the transfiguration. The attestation by
Moses and Elijah ("law and prophets") and the
dazzling perception of "his glory" by his disciples
validate and confirm Peter's confession, "[You
are] the Messiah of God" (Luke 9:20).

Compare this word from heaven with that in
Luke 3:21–22.

PRAYER: Like Peter, I hardly know what to do or
say when I glimpse your wondrous glory, Lord.
Lead me into a more adequate apprehension of
who you are, and teach me to respond with praise
and adoration. Amen.

"Astounded at the Greatness of God"
READ Luke 9:37–45

But Jesus rebuked the unclean spirit, healed
the boy, and gave him back to his father.
And all were astounded at the greatness
of God.

Luke 9:42b–43a

However great, our Lord is never aloof. That
which is experienced on the mountaintop is put
to work in the valley. The greatness of glory on the
heights of revelation now mixes with the ugliness
of the human condition and brings a beautiful
peace.

Why were the disciples unable to help the man
and his boy?

PRAYER: What a glorious ministry you bring to
me, Jesus! You take my faithlessness and frustration and create something firm and sure. You
don't reject me because I am inadequate, but accept me and make me adequate. Thank you. *Amen.*

"The Least Among All"
READ Luke 9:46–48

"Whoever welcomes this child in my name
    welcomes me, and whoever welcomes
    me welcomes the one who sent me; for
    the least among all of you is the
    greatest."

Luke 9:48

Jesus uses a child as an object lesson: leadership in the kingdom means putting yourself on a level with the least important people and serving them in the name of Christ. It is not making "big" decisions or associating with the "great."

Do you have an ambition that gets in the way of your service?

PRAYER: My pride keeps asserting itself, God. I keep pushing to be in front instead of quietly working behind the scenes to make your word effective and personal. Forgive my arrogance; train me in servant skills. *Amen.*

"Do Not Stop Him"

READ Luke 9:49–50

But Jesus said to him, "Do not stop him;
for whoever is not against you is for you."

Luke 9:50

Why are we more eager to set up rivalries than to develop alliances? Jesus warns against rejecting allies in kingdom work just because they aren't in "our church" or don't speak "our language." He helps us see beneath the surface differences that separate us and to discern the deeper unities that the gospel creates.

Who are some of your allies in the faith?

PRAYER: Give me, Lord, the kind of sharp insight that sees the unnoticed, obscure good that others are doing and discovers the common ground of obedience beneath diversities of custom and style. *Amen.*

"Rebuked Them"

READ Luke 9:51–56

But he turned and rebuked them.

Luke 9:55

It is difficult, having discovered that all the glorious energies of God are focused in Jesus, to acknowledge that his chosen way also involves suffering, death, and resurrection. Both the Samaritans and the disciples wanted only part of Jesus. But we cannot pick and choose— if we confess him as our Savior, we must also accept him as our Lord.

What did the Samaritans reject in Jesus? What did the disciples reject?

PRAYER: I am more quick to accept your help, Jesus, than to submit to your way. Rebuke me when I drag my feet or argue. Forgive me for all the times I try to separate my belief in you from your way of life. Amen.

"I Will Follow You"

READ Luke 9:57–62

As they were going along the road,
  someone said to him, "I will follow you
  wherever you go."

Luke 9:57

Following Jesus does not ensure an easier way
of life—it is not a free ride on Christ's coattails.
Discipleship carries with it neither comforts nor
conveniences.

What inconveniences have you encountered as
a follower of Jesus?

PRAYER: Lord Jesus, I would follow you not to escape onerous tasks but because you are the way to
eternal life. Grant that I may be neither deflected
from my aim nor distracted from my decision.
Amen.

"Carry No Purse"

READ Luke 10:1–16

"Carry no purse, no bag, no sandals; and
greet no one on the road."

Luke 10:4

The work of God's kingdom is not accomplished
by what we bring to the task. Neither our money
nor our geniality brings in the kingdom. Our
Lord needs us to be obedient disciples, doing his
work and rejoicing in his grace.

Why does Jesus instruct the disciples to "travel
light"?

PRAYER: Let all my skill be to know your will, O
Christ, to obey your commands, to rejoice in your
presence. Help me to set aside the sins that cling
so closely and then to run with perseverance the
race you have set before me (Hebrews 12:1).
Amen.

"I Watched Satan Fall"
READ Luke 10:17–20

He said to them, "I watched Satan fall from
heaven like a flash of lightning."

Luke 10:18

The theme of the gospel story does not consist in
what we do to put down evil, but in what God
does to make us right with him. It is not our spiritual warfare that holds center stage in the drama
of redemption, but Christ's.

What are some implications of Satan's fall?

PRAYER: "Thy mighty name salvation is, And keeps
my happy soul above: Comfort it brings, and
power, and peace, And joy, and everlasting love: To
me, with Thy great name, are given Pardon and
holiness and heaven" (Charles Wesley, "Thou
Hidden Source of Calm Repose"). *Amen.*

"Prophets and Kings Desired to See"
READ Luke 10:21–24

"For I tell you that many prophets and
kings desired to see what you see, but
did not see it, and to hear what you
hear, but did not hear it."

Luke 10:24

People who want their eyes dazzled with won
drous sights and their ears charmed with exotic
sounds need to know that the greatest privilege
any person can have is to hear God's word spoken
in the clear, gracious message of Jesus Christ.

Who are some of the "prophets and kings"
Jesus refers to?

PRAYER: "Open my eyes, that I may see Glimpses
of truth Thou hast for me; Place in my hands the
wonderful key That shall unclasp, and set me free.
Silently now I wait for Thee, Ready, my God, Thy
will to see; Open my eyes illumine me, Spirit
divine!" (Clara H. Scott, "Open My Eyes, that I
May See"). Amen.

"Love"

> He answered, "You shall love the Lord your
> God with all your heart, and with all
> your soul, and with all your strength,
> and with all your mind; and your
> neighbor as yourself."
>
> Luke 10:27

The lawyer's question, conceived in a spirit of contention, sought to exclude and limit. It produced, by the grace of Jesus, an answer that embraces every person. The double command (love your God; love your neighbor) centers all action for the Christian.

Whom do you have a hard time recognizing as your neighbor?

PRAYER: God, my love is meager and fickle; yours is vast and constant. Now that you have told me, unforgettably, who my neighbor is, pour out your love on me so that I may love my neighbor "as I ought to love" (George Croly, "Spirit of God, Descend Upon My Heart"). In Jesus' name. *Amen.*

MARCH 28

"Only One Thing"
READ Luke 10:38–42

But the Lord answered her, "Martha, Martha,
you are worried and distracted by many
things; there is need of only one thing.
Mary has chosen the better part, which
will not be taken away from her."

Luke 10:41–42

Our Lord is not a despot who sends us on the
errands that he considers beneath his dignity, but
a companion who invites us to share his work
with him. He is not nearly as interested that we
work for him as that we *be with* him.

Are you more like Martha or Mary?

PRAYER: Lord, for a few minutes today I will simply wait at your feet, quietly listening, attentively
believing. Show me the "need of only one thing,"
for your name's sake. *Amen.*

"Teach Us to Pray"

READ Luke 11:1–13

> He was praying in a certain place, and after
> he had finished, one of his disciples said
> to him, "Lord, teach us to pray, as John
> taught his disciples."
>
> Luke 11:1

The prayer Jesus used as a model to teach us to pray is warmly personal, succinct, and direct. It is a remarkable concentration of the essential relations between human beings and God. Jesus, more than any other, can teach us to pray.

What phrase in the Lord's Prayer will you concentrate on today?

PRAYER: Father, guard me from long-windedness and speech making in my prayers. I aspire not to a flowery eloquence but to a direct simplicity. Keep all my words with you honest, for Jesus' sake. *Amen.*

"By the Finger of God"
READ Luke 11:14–28

"But if it is by the finger of God that I cast
out the demons, then the kingdom of
God has come to you."

Luke 11:20

The illustration is arresting: Jesus compares himself to a robber who plunders Satan's house of all
its possessions. Everything and everyone in the
world is in "danger" of being stolen back by
Christ. Poor Satan!

What is the evidence of Jesus' authority?

PRAYER: All praise to you, Father, for your kingdom come. I see the people and possessions of
this world change hands, from Satan's bondage to
Christ's rule. I celebrate your power and your
peace. Amen.

"The Sign of Jonah"

READ Luke 11:29–36

> "For just as Jonah became a sign to the
> people of Nineveh, so the Son of Man
> will be to this generation."

Luke 11:30

There is a religious curiosity, common in every age, that does more harm than good. It is interested in entertainment instead of holiness, in diversion instead of discipleship. Jesus refused to indulge it, and warns us of such "light," which only plunges us into a deeper darkness.

What is the sign of Jonah?

PRAYER: "I take, O Cross, thy shadow For my abiding place: I ask no other sunshine than The sunshine of His face; Content to let the world go by, To know no gain nor loss: My sinful self my only shame, My glory all, the cross" (Elizabeth C. Clephane, "Beneath the Cross of Jesus"). Amen.

APRIL 1

"You Fools!"

READ Luke 11:37–44

"You fools! Did not the one who made the
outside make the inside also?"

Luke 11:40

It is easy enough to learn the habits of religion—
a style of dress, a distinctive vocabulary, a set of
traditions. And it is easy, having acquired the
habits, to suppose that God is pleased. But he
could not care less. He is interested in us, not in
our "religion," so called.

What were some of the Pharisaic habits? What
are some of your habits?

PRAYER: Lord, I don't want just to go through the
motions today. I know that would satisfy the
people around me, at least some of them, but it
wouldn't satisfy you. Draw me close to you in a
living faith, burning with love for my Savior.
Amen.

"Woe Also to You Lawyers!"
READ Luke 11:45–54

And he said, "Woe also to you lawyers! For
   you load people with burdens hard to
   bear, and you yourselves do not lift a
   finger to ease them."

Luke 11:46

A teacher, and especially a teacher of the faith,
must experiment with all truth—and not simply
in the laboratory or the lecture hall but in his or
her daily living. Each truth must be faced with the
question, "Can I live it?" Jesus, who lived every
detail he taught, has only scorn for those who
merely talk truth.

Why was Jesus angry with the lawyers?

PRAYER: Dear Lord, I know that every word you
speak to me has been validated by the lived reality
of your crucifixion and resurrection. Give me
courage to live your truths personally and intensely through the ordinary hours of this day.
Amen.

"Hypocrisy"

READ Luke 12:1–3

Meanwhile, when the crowd gathered by
the thousands, so that they trampled on
one another, he began to speak first to
his disciples, "Beware of the yeast of the
Pharisees, that is, their hypocrisy."

Luke 12:1

The hypocrite is a most dangerous person—more
so than the drunken driver on the highway or the
psychopath on the street. By falsifying the truth of
the inner life, the hypocrite bewilders and embit-
ters the lives of those who hunger for eternal life
and search for the reality of God.

How is hypocrisy like leaven?

PRAYER: O God, I welcome your word, which is
sharp to lay bare every thought and intention in
my heart. Root out all hypocrisy and cultivate
honesty in me, in the name of Jesus Christ. Amen.

"Even the Hairs of Your Head"

READ Luke 12:4–7

"But even the hairs of your head are all
counted. Do not be afraid; you are of
more value than many sparrows."

Luke 12:7

If we suppose that the universe is hostile to us, we will spend all our energy protecting ourselves from misadventure, defending ourselves against malign forces. But if we know that the God of heaven and earth is concerned about us, we are free to live expressively, openly, and fearlessly in the world.

What fears can you dismiss on the basis of Jesus' words?

PRAYER: I rest confidently and fearlessly in your love, dear God. Whatever happens to me this day, I know that it will not separate me from your love. I will give myself to living boldly in love for the sake of my Lord and Savior, Jesus Christ. *Amen.*

"What You Ought to Say"

READ Luke 12:8–12

". . . for the Holy Spirit will teach you at
that very hour what you ought to say."

Luke 12:12

Denials are an attempt to exclude God's presence;
blasphemies are an attempt to pervert his purposes
(to damnation rather than salvation). Our proper
speech is in the form of confession, which affirms
God's presence and submits to his purposes.

Who teaches us to speak rightly of Christ?

PRAYER: Keep my speech, O God, especially when
I am speaking of you, from the blusters of denial,
the irreverence of blasphemy, and the stuttering of
anxiety. Enable me to speak simply and directly of
the Lord who is all in all to me, even Jesus Christ.
Amen.

"Not Rich Toward God"

READ Luke 12:13–21

"So it is with those who store up treasures
for themselves but are not rich toward
God."

Luke 12:21

Jesus clarifies a basic decision each of us must make: Will we concentrate on "getting ahead" or on "getting with God"? Will we use our energy to develop lively, loving relationships with our neighbor and with God? Or will we use it to fill a bigger barn? (of which it can be said, as Oscar Wilde once described a mackerel in the moonlight, "It glitters but it stinks").

What makes a person "rich toward God"?

PRAYER: "Riches I heed not, nor man's empty praise, Thou mine inheritance, now and always; Thou and Thou only, first in my heart, High King of heaven, my Treasure Thou art" (Mary Byrne, trans., "Be Thou My Vision," ancient Irish hymn). *Amen.*

"Do Not Worry"
READ Luke 12:22–31

He said to his disciples, "Therefore I tell you,
do not worry about your life, what you
will eat, or about your body, what you
will wear."

Luke 12:22

Worry or anxiety is a common consequence of
pride. The proud man insists on running his own
life. But he is no good at it. As evidence of his in-
competence piles up, he becomes more and more
nervous. The woman of faith turns the running of
her life over to God. And as evidence of God's
compassion and competence accumulates, she ac-
quires serenity.

What do you learn from observations on ravens
and lilies?

PRAYER: God, I cannot handle my mind, nor my
emotions, nor my money. I turn them over to
you. You are the Creator and I am the creature;
you are the Lover and I am the beloved. Rule my
spirit in wisdom and order my ways in love. Amen.

"Your Father's Good Pleasure"
READ Luke 12:32–34

"Do not be afraid, little flock, for it is your
Father's good pleasure to give you the
kingdom."

Luke 12:32

As long as we view life as getting and achieving
we are subject to anxieties, for no fortress is
strong enough to protect us from loss and no retreat remote enough to separate us from threat.
But if life consists in giving and praising, there is
nothing that can be taken from us that has not already been given up, and no danger that has not
already been dissipated by the cross.

Where is your treasure?

PRAYER: Father, I accept your counsel. I take all the
plunder I have been holding avariciously—things
and ideas, ambitions and entertainments, people
and places—and set them before you as an offering to be used for your purposes, in Jesus Christ.
Amen.

"Like Those Who Are Waiting"
READ Luke 12:35–40

". . . be like those who are waiting for their
master to return from the wedding
banquet, so that they may open the door
for him as soon as he comes and
knocks."

Luke 12:36

We are living in the very early stages of eternity.
Alert Christians never know what God is going to
do next. They do know, though, that it will be
good, for it will be done in and through Jesus
Christ.

How does a Christian keep his or her "lamps
burning"?

PRAYER: Father, what marvelous things you must
have planned for the days ahead! Help me not to
become so engrossed in what has already happened that I fail to be open to what you have yet
to do with me. Above all, keep me alert for the return of Jesus Christ in all power and glory. Amen.

"To Whom Much Has Been Given"
READ Luke 12:41–48

"But the one who did not know and did
what deserved a beating will receive a
light beating. From everyone to whom
much has been given, much will be
required; and from the one to whom
much has been entrusted, even more
will be demanded.

Luke 12:48

Life, and especially the Christian life, is a gift to
be used in generous service, not a privilege to be
squandered indulgently or hardened selfishly.
God's blessings are designed to be shared in responsible love, not dissipated in capricious lust.

What has been committed to you?

PRAYER: "Take my hands, and let them move At
the impulse of Thy love. Take my feet, and let
them be Swift and beautiful for Thee. Take my
voice, and let me sing, Always, only, for my King.
Take my lips, and let them be Filled with messages
from Thee" (Frances Ridley Havergal, "Take My
Life, and Let It Be Consecrated"). *Amen.*

APRIL 11

"Divided"

READ Luke 12:49–53

"From now on five in one household will
be divided, three against two and two
against three. . . ."

Luke 12:52

Jesus is a crossroads—he clarifies alternatives.
Will we choose God's peace? Will we join the
community of God's people? Decisions must be
made. In the process of saying yes to God, we
have to say no to anyone or anything that is
defiant of, or a substitute for, God.

What divisions has a decision for Christ produced in your life?

PRAYER: God give me the courage to follow
through on my decisions for you. Give me the
strength to say no to anything or anyone that
would dilute my yes to you. Amen.

"It Is Going to Rain"

READ Luke 12:54–56

He also said to the crowds, "When you see a cloud rising in the west, you immediately say, 'It is going to rain'; and so it happens."

Luke 12:54

Everyone, it seems, is an expert on the weather. We are quick to observe and ready to predict. Why will we not be as observant of the weather of the "present time"? Perhaps because we know that our observations will require follow-through decisions, that something more than umbrellas and raincoats is needed—something like repentance.

What are some signs of Christ's coming?

PRAYER: Lord Jesus Christ, I walk preoccupied with eyes downward: I miss the signs and the songs. Open my eyes to the unmistakable buds of grace, my ears to the clear notes of hope so that I can be alive to the full reality of your salvation in this world. *Amen.*

"Settle the Case"

READ Luke 12:57–59

"Thus, when you go with your accuser
before a magistrate, on the way make an
effort to settle the case, or you may be
dragged before the judge, and the judge
hand you over to the officer, and the
officer throw you in prison."

Luke 12:58

If we put as much effort into getting right with
people as in getting even with them or getting
ahead of them, we would do a better job of putting
our Lord's counsel on love and justice into action.
Right relations are not matters we can refer to
judges to establish for us; they are present tasks to
be achieved through us.

Whom are you having trouble getting along
with?

PRAYER: God, you give me brothers and sisters to
live with, but I do not always get along with
them. Our wills collide, our needs crisscross, our
demands clash. If I cannot get along with them
naturally, help me to do it supernaturally, so that I
may live in friendly justice with my neighbors, in
Jesus' name. Amen.

"Unless You Repent"

READ Luke 13:1–5

"No, I tell you; but unless you repent, you
will all perish just as they did."

Luke 13:5

Do we suppose that when people perish or suffer
in some extraordinary way they must have been
guilty of some extraordinary sin? Not so, says
Jesus. We all face the same judgment, whether it
gets into the newspapers or not. We, therefore,
must all repent.

Who do you think is more wicked than you
yourself?

PRAYER: Help me, gracious God, to realize the
gravity of my own sins, to turn to you daily for
forgiveness, and then to live consciously and con-
tinuously by your mercy in Jesus Christ. *Amen.*

"Sir, Let It Alone"

READ Luke 13:6–9

> "He replied, 'Sir, let it alone for one more
> year, until I dig around it and put manure
> on it. If it bears fruit next year, well and
> good; but if not, you can cut it down.'"
>
> Luke 13:8–9

Unproductive and unpromising as we are, Jesus
intercedes for us: he gives us more time, another
chance, fresh opportunities for fruitfulness. Will
we presume upon his grace and live indifferently?
Or will we seize the day for repentance and live as
disciples? Will we squander or redeem the time?

What in you needs cultivating?

PRAYER: O God, break up the fallow ground in my
life and sow works of repentance, so that in the
time of your visitation there will be a harvest of
spirit fruit for your gathering. Amen.

"*Woman, You Are Set Free*"
READ Luke 13:10–17

> When Jesus saw her, he called her over and
> said, "Woman, you are set free from
> your ailment."
>
> Luke 13:12

We, like the Pharisees, are ingenious at finding religious reasons for our disobedience. By keeping a "higher law" we exempt ourselves from responding to neighbors in need. Association with Jesus, though, makes that kind of pious disobedience impossible.

Do you ever give "Christian" reasons for avoiding God's clear command?

PRAYER: Too much of my life, Lord, is like the Pharisees'. I manage to keep up right appearances and fulfill obligations while I sidestep obvious opportunities for compassion. Forgive me for hiding behind religious forms; help me to be in touch with persons in need. *Amen.*

"Like a Mustard Seed"
READ Luke 13:18–21

> "It is like a mustard seed that someone
> took and sowed in the garden; it grew
> and became a tree, and the birds of the
> air made nests in its branches."

Luke 13:19

God's way, it seems, is to begin small: in an obscure Middle Eastern nation, in a Bethlehem stable . . . and in me. Mustard seed. Leaven. But each of these inconspicuous beginnings has vast, eternal consequences.

Recall times when you have mistaken size for significance.

PRAYER: God, when the noisy affairs of the world distract me, recall to my conscience these mustard seed and leaven parables. I put my trust not in size but in your word, which brings worlds into being and prepares me for eternal habitations. *Amen.*

"The Narrow Door"

READ Luke 13:22–30

"Strive to enter through the narrow door;
   for many, I tell you, will try to enter and
   will not be able."

Luke 13:24

The kingdom of God excludes no one by reason of birth or background ("people will come from east and west, from north and south"; v. 29). At the same time it includes no one merely because of vague associations with Jesus ("you taught in our streets"; v. 26). The "narrow door" is both an open invitation and a focused goal.

Who are some of the "last who will be first"?

PRAYER: "Jesus, lead the way Through our life's long day, And with faithful footsteps steady, We will follow, ever ready. Guide us by Thy hand To the Fatherland" (Nicolaus L. von Zinzendorf, "Jesus, Lead the Way"). *Amen.*

"Kills the Prophets"
READ Luke 13:31–35

> "Jerusalem, Jerusalem, the city that kills
> the prophets and stones those who are
> sent to it! How often have I desired to
> gather your children together as a hen
> gathers her brood under her wings, and
> you were not willing!"
>
> Luke 13:34

The difficulties of the road did not deter our Lord: to malicious Herod he was boldly contemptuous; to mercurial Jerusalem he was mercifully compassionate. With such a combination of bravery and gentleness Jesus makes his way through our lives to establish the kingdom of God among us.

Why did the Pharisees warn Jesus?

PRAYER: Guide me, God, through every peril. Protect me from the designs of the enemy and equip me for loving the uncommitted, so that I may follow in your steps with good hope and steady faith. In Jesus' name. Amen.

"Sabbath"

READ Luke 14:1–6

Then he said to them, "If one of you has a
child or an ox that has fallen into a well,
will you not immediately pull it out on a
sabbath day?"

Luke 14:5

Jesus rescued the sabbath day from jailhouse
conditions in which one could barely move for
fear of breaking a ritual regulation or offending a
pious Pharisee, and made it a celebrative day in
which a person could freely and spontaneously
express love for both God and neighbor.

How do you observe the sabbath?

PRAYER: "I pray, O God, for all human hearts that
today are lifted up to Thee in earnest desire, and
for every group of men and women who are met
together to praise and magnify Thy name. Whatever be their mode of worship, be graciously
pleased to accept their humble offices of prayer
and praise, and lead them unto life eternal,
through Jesus Christ our Lord" (John Baillie, *A
Diary of Prayer*). *Amen.*

"Friend, Move Up Higher"
READ Luke 14:7–11

"But when you are invited, go and sit
down at the lowest place, so that when
your host comes, he may say to you,
'Friend, move up higher'; then you will
be honored in the presence of all who
sit at the table with you."

Luke 14:10

Humility is full of surprises—every advance,
every compliment, every recognition is an unex-
pected pleasure. Pride, on the other hand, is liable
to shameful disappointments. God knows our
true worth and our proper position, and he will
finally place us where he wants us.

Why is pride so dangerous to the Christian?

PRAYER: Deliver me, O God, from a false humility that denies your gifts and from an assertive
pride that denies your lordship. Help me to see
myself as you see me, to accept my limitations
and use my abilities to the glory of your name.
Amen.

"Invite the Poor"
READ Luke 14:12–14

> "But when you give a banquet, invite the
> poor, the crippled, the lame, and the
> blind."
>
> Luke 14:13

Christ challenges our social behavior: Do we surround ourselves with people whose position and reputation will somehow make us more significant? Or do we develop a strategy by which we can share what we are and have in gracious and generous friendship?

What is your relationship with those who have less than you?

PRAYER: I want to live with others the way you, dear Lord, lived among human beings, not calculating friendships on the basis of what I can get out of them but simply looking for ways in which I can share what you have given me. In the name of Jesus. *Amen.*

"Excuses"

READ Luke 14:15–24

"But they all alike began to make excuses.
The first said to him, 'I have bought a
piece of land, and I must go out and see
it; please accept my regrets.' Another
said, 'I have bought five yoke of oxen,
and I am going to try them out; please
accept my regrets.' Another said, 'I have
just been married, and therefore I
cannot come.'"

Luke 14:18–20

God invites us to a glorious life of feasting and
joyful celebration. Our excuses reveal an astonish-
ing preference for "fields," "oxen," and "wives"—
all legitimate in themselves, but not in any way to
be compared with an invitation to God's banquet.
The good is the enemy of the best.

Which excuse have you used?

PRAYER: I don't want anything to stand in the way
of saying an immediate yes to you, O God—not
the requirements of work, not the necessities of
family, not the demands of society. I want your
presence and your love beyond all else, through
Jesus Christ. Amen.

"Give Up All Your Possessions"
READ Luke 14:25–33

> "So therefore, none of you can become my
> disciple if you do not give up all your
> possessions."
>
> Luke 14:33

Renunciation does not usher in a life of austerity
in which we live meagerly and poorly; it is the act
that releases everything we have and are for use by
God in the munificent life of the kingdom of God.

What does "give up all your possessions" mean
to you?

PRAYER: "Almighty God, grant us purity of heart
and strength of purpose, that no selfish passion
may hinder us from knowing Thy will, no weakness from doing it; that in Thy light we may see
light clearly, and in Thy service find perfect freedom, for Jesus' sake" (Book of Common Worship).
Amen.

APRIL 25

"Salt"

READ Luke 14:34–35

> "Salt is good; but if salt has lost its taste,
>   how can its saltiness be restored?"
>
> Luke 14:34

The Christian, like salt, has no particular value externally, no formal beauty, no usefulness as a thing in itself. Usefulness derives from a nature that, in relation to others, preserves and enhances. If we have no inner life "in Christ," we are worthless.

How are you like salt?

PRAYER: Dear God, make me a salty Christian; use me quietly and inconspicuously among the people with whom I live to release the flavor of joy, to enhance the quality of peace, to preserve the life of love, through Jesus Christ. Amen.

APRIL 26

"Grumbling"
READ Luke 15:1–7

And the Pharisees and the scribes were
grumbling and saying, "This fellow
welcomes sinners and eats with them."
Luke 15:2

The Pharisees misunderstood completely: they
thought God's kingdom was an exclusive club to
which men and women were admitted when they
became adequately righteous. Jesus showed it was
more like a search party, invading the world, seeking to share God's beneficent rule with everyone.

How does the parable change your ideas about
God?

PRAYER: How miserable I would be, O God, if you
paid attention only to the insiders. How wonderful it is that you go out of your way to share love
with the outsiders. Thank you, in Jesus' name.
Amen.

APRIL 27

"Carefully"

READ Luke 15:8–10

"Or what woman having ten silver coins, if
she loses one of them, does not light a
lamp, sweep the house, and search
carefully until she finds it?"

Luke 15:8

The parable tells us a most glorious thing about
our condition before God. Our "lostness," far
from removing us from his concern, actually
focuses it. Our separation from God sets in motion a massive search operation in which God
through Christ seeks to restore us to fellowship
with himself.

How does the parable change your ideas about
non-Christians?

PRAYER: Thank you, O God, for your diligence.
The immense value you place on each of your
children, the persevering search that tirelessly
seeks each one out—all of this makes it possible
for me to no longer cry "I'm lost," but to sing
"I'm found!" *Amen.*

"Alive Again"
READ Luke 15:11–24

"But the father said to his slaves, 'Quickly,
bring out a robe—the best one—and
put it on him; put a ring on his finger
and sandals on his feet. And get the
fatted calf and kill it, and let us eat and
celebrate; for this son of mine was dead
and is alive again; he was lost and is
found!' And they began to celebrate."

Luke 15:22–24

The story tells us how God looks on us when we
run away from him, wasting his gifts and forget-
ting his love. He neither reviles nor disowns us;
he waits for us. He waits for our repentance, out
of which he makes a personal resurrection. "This
son of mine was dead and is alive again."

What is the key phrase in the parable?

PRAYER: I praise your great name, O God! How
many hopeless lives you have turned into victories!
How many prodigals you have received in triumph! How much rejection has become redemption! How much of what looked like death has
become by your grace new life! All praise to the
risen Christ! *Amen.*

"His Elder Son"

"But he answered his father, 'Listen! For all
these years I have been working like a
slave for you, and I have never disobeyed
your command; yet you have never
given me even a young goat so that I
might celebrate with my friends.'"

Luke 15:29

The elder brother was separated from his father's
joy by an icy self-righteousness. We can, it seems,
be as lost to God through priggishness and pride
as through profligate living among the harlots of
the "distant country."

Are you more like the younger or the elder son?

PRAYER: Forbid it, God, that any responsible living that I engage in today should separate me
from your grace, or lead me to think that I am no
longer in need of forgiveness. Through Jesus
Christ my Lord and Savior. Amen.

"Acted Shrewdly"

READ Luke 16:1–9

> "And his master commended the dishonest
> manager because he had acted shrewdly;
> for the children of this age are more
> shrewd in dealing with their own
> generation than are the children of
> light."

Luke 16:8

Jesus commends the steward not for his dishonesty but for his shrewdness. Faced with a crisis that meant utter ruin to him, the man realized the seriousness of his position, did some strenuous thinking, and found the means of coping with the situation. In such ways Jesus urges the hesitant and the wavering to take seriously the crisis of the kingdom of God.

How are you like the steward?

PRAYER: God, don't let me lazily slide along through life taking the course of least resistance. I want to face the crisis that your love presents to me with all the intelligence and all the faith at my disposal. For Jesus' sake. Amen.

"Lovers of Money"
READ Luke 16:10–15

> The Pharisees, who were lovers of money,
> heard all this, and they ridiculed him. So
> he said to them, "You are those who
> justify yourselves in the sight of others;
> but God knows your hearts; for what is
> prized by human beings is an
> abomination in the sight of God."
>
> Luke 16:14–15

We suppose, in our naïveté, that rich people are
especially blessed. How else would they have got-
ten so rich? Riches are more likely to be evidence
of an idolatrous devotion to mammon—a preference for things over people and for getting over
giving.

Do you ever envy the rich?

PRAYER: O God, you know how attached I can become to money and material things. Free me from
such bondage. Help me to understand that I am
never an owner and always a steward. Amen.

"One Stroke of the Law"
READ Luke 16:16–18

> "But it is easier for heaven and earth to
> pass away, than for one stroke of a letter
> in the law to be dropped."
>
> Luke 16:17

It is possible for "the law and the prophets" to degenerate into legal bondage and oppressive do-goodism. And then we are tempted to throw them out and start all over. But God does not throw out, he renovates; he does not eliminate, he completes. All his words and deeds are fulfilled in the Word made flesh (John 1:14).

What part of the law would you like to get rid of?

PRAYER: Complete "the law and the prophets" in me, Almighty God. Take what is half-understood and halfheartedly obeyed and make a whole faith from it. Take the fragments of religion that I have collected through the years and make a whole person of me, in Christ. *Amen.*

"A Poor Man Named Lazarus"
READ Luke 16:19–31

"And at his gate lay a poor man named
Lazarus, covered with sores, who longed
to satisfy his hunger with what fell from
the rich man's table; even the dogs
would come and lick his sores."

Luke 16:20–21

Standard religious thinking in Jesus' day interpreted the poverty and suffering of one like Lazarus as
a sign of God's displeasure. Jesus holds him up as
a victim of humankind's cruel indifference and
calls us to a compassion that imitates God's love
for the needy.

How do you express your concern for the poor?

PRAYER: Use the story of Lazarus in my life, O
God, to keep me sensitive to human need wherever it may occur, to keep me aware of the high
regard you have for the poor and the suffering,
and to increase compassion in all my thoughts
and actions. In Jesus' name. *Amen.*

"You Must Forgive"
READ Luke 17:1–6

> "And if the same person sins against you
>   seven times a day, and turns back to
>   you seven times and says, 'I repent,'
>   you must forgive."

Luke 17:4

The nexus of all relationships between human beings (as in all relationships between God and human beings) is the act of forgiveness. Without it, neither love nor joy nor peace can mature.

How does Jesus emphasize the necessity for forgiveness?

PRAYER: Dear God, let no resentment against others find root in my life today, no critical spirit put distance between me and those I have been given to love, no wrong (whether fancied or real) be allowed to bear evil fruit in me. I will seek to both give and receive forgiveness, even as I have been forgiven in Jesus Christ. *Amen.*

"What We Ought to Have Done"

READ Luke 17:7–10

> "So you also, when you have done all that
> you were ordered to do, say, 'We are
> worthless slaves; we have done only
> what we ought to have done!'"

Luke 17:10

The Christian is not called to grand heroics, but to common discipleship. We are not set apart for privilege, to be looked at in awe by others simply because we believe, but commanded to simple faith through the daily round.

Do you sometimes think you have privileges with God because of your faith?

PRAYER: "I bind my heart in thrall To the God, the Lord of all, To the God, the poor man's Friend, And the Christ whom He did send. I bind myself to peace, To make strife and envy cease, God, knit Thou sure the cord Of my thralldom to my Lord!" (Lauchlan MacLean Watt, "I Bind My Heart This Tide"). Amen.

"Where Are They?"
READ Luke 17:11–19

Then Jesus asked, "Were not ten made clean?
But the other nine, where are they?"

Luke 17:17

As a sequel to the story of the Good Samaritan
(Luke 10:29–37), Luke gives us the story of the
Grateful Samaritan. The first is a model for responding to human need; the second, a model for
responding to God's grace. Gratitude completes
the work of Christ in our lives by giving it expression in praise and pilgrimage.

What recent gift have you failed to give thanks
for?

PRAYER: "Almighty and merciful Father . . . grant
unto us with Thy gifts a heart to love Thee; and
enable us to show our thankfulness for all Thy
benefits; by giving up ourselves to Thy service,
and delighting in all things to do Thy blessed will,
through Jesus Christ our Lord" (Book of Common
Worship). Amen.

"Among You"

READ Luke 17:20–21

". . . nor will they say, 'Look, here it is!' or
'There it is!' For, in fact, the kingdom of
God is among you."

Luke 17:21

The kingdom of God is not for looking at, but for
living in. It cannot be examined through a tele-
scope from afar, nor analyzed up close through a
microscope. It can only be "entered." Only those
who love, hope, and believe in the name of Jesus
experience the kingdom.

How do you participate in the kingdom?

PRAYER: Father, deliver me from the idle curiosity
that wants to know about your kingdom. I don't
want to be a spectator to your love, but a child of
your love, even as you have shown me in Jesus
Christ. Amen.

"The Days of Noah"
READ Luke 17:22–37

"Just as it was in the days of Noah, so too
it will be in the days of the Son of Man."
Luke 17:26

"Those who are unwilling to live by faith, and who tamper with signs and programs and dates, are to be resolutely avoided. When the Kingdom finally comes, it will come as suddenly and decisively as lightening, and all will know it. In the meantime, believers must live in constant expectancy and readiness" (Donald G. Miller, Luke. Layman's Bible Commentary Series, vol. 18. [Louisville, KY: John Knox Press, 1959]).

How are these days like the days of Noah?

PRAYER: O God, save me from the confusion of mind that alarmist doomsdayers inflict; but also from the carelessness of heart that comes from shirked prayers; in the name of him who is coming again. *Amen.*

"Quickly Grant Justice"
READ Luke 18:1–8

"I tell you, he will quickly grant justice to
   them. And yet, when the Son of Man
   comes, will he find faith on earth?"

Luke 18:8

Do we suppose that God is reluctant to answer
our prayers? Do we attribute habits of procrastination to him? Do we imagine him indifferent to
our anguish? Jesus knows God better than we do,
and he shares that better knowledge with us, as-
suring us that God will vindicate his people who
pray and hope.

What do you want God to do for you?

PRAYER: Father, you know how quickly I become
discouraged. I interpret every delay as defeat. I
think every silence is a sign of indifference. Give
me grace always to pray and not lose heart, as I
wait for your speedy vindication in Jesus Christ.
Amen.

"Some Who Trusted in Themselves"
READ Luke 18:9–14

He also told this parable to some who
trusted in themselves that they were
righteous and regarded others with
contempt. . . .

Luke 18:9

The moment prayer becomes a means of putting
our best behavior on display before God (and,
not-so-incidentally, our neighbors), it is a parody
of prayer. Prayer is not a device by which we call
God's attention to ourselves but the way in which
we become attentive to God.

Contrast the two prayers in the parable.

PRAYER: O God, I need this parable; I need the
warning over and over. Teach me to pray in humility, honestly telling my needs, and my ingratitude; freely singing my joy. Amen.

"Let the Little Children Come"
READ Luke 18:15–17

But Jesus called for them and said, "Let the
little children come to me, and do not
stop them; for it is to such as these that
the kingdom of God belongs."

Luke 18:16

Human beings are always trying to turn the kingdom of God into an exclusive club for people like
themselves. Jesus, in contrast, opens it to the
lowly, the inquiring, the growing—the mass of
humanity of which children are such delightful
representatives.

What does it mean to enter "as a little child"?

PRAYER: When I come to you, Lord, as a "know-
it-all," I feel your rebuke; when I come as a child
with openness, delight, and wide-eyed expectancy, I sense your blessing. Lead me in the path of
your blessing. Amen.

"Still One Thing Lacking"
READ Luke 18:18–30

When Jesus heard this, he said to him,
  "There is still one thing lacking. Sell all
  that you own and distribute the money
  to the poor, and you will have treasure
  in heaven; then come, follow me."

Luke 18:22

The rich ruler is a baffling figure: a person who was extraordinarily religious but whose religion was put to selfish uses. For him religion was all on the outside, observing commandments and acquiring a reputation, rather than an inner commitment and a personal discipleship.

Why are riches so dangerous to discipleship?

PRAYER: Lord, what one thing do I lack? Examine my heart and show me if there is some basic selfishness that stands between me and you. *Amen.*

MAY 13

"Going up to Jerusalem"
READ Luke 18:31–34

Then he took the twelve aside and said
to them, "See, we are going up to
Jerusalem, and everything that is written
about the Son of Man by the prophets
will be accomplished."

Luke 18:31

Our minds are highly resistant to suggestions of sacrifice and suffering. We want to take shortcuts to eternity, avoiding the road "up to Jerusalem" that is so carefully mapped out and pioneered by Jesus.

Why did the disciples not understand?

PRAYER: Lord Jesus Christ, I will follow where you lead. Perhaps I will never understand the way of the cross; I will, though, by your grace, learn to walk in it, confident that since it is the way you chose, it is my way to the Father. Amen.

"Have Mercy on Me!"

READ Luke 18:35–43

Then he shouted, "Jesus, Son of David,
    have mercy on me!"

Luke 18:38

The blind man didn't complain to Jesus about the horrible miscarriage of justice that had left him blind while worse men enjoyed their sight; nor did he whiningly beg for a few pennies to get him through another day. His prayer was a full-throated shout for mercy. He wanted neither "answers" nor "alms" but wholeness—and he knew who could give it to him.

What do you want from Jesus?

PRAYER: Thank you, merciful God, for taking my cries for help so seriously, for listening so carefully to me, and for calling me into your presence for healing and salvation. *Amen.*

"Zacchaeus"

READ Luke 19:1–10

A man was there named Zacchaeus; he was
a chief tax collector and was rich.

Luke 19:2

No one—no matter how small, no matter how in-
famous—is overlooked by God. Neither insignifi-
cance nor sin cuts us off from God's attention.
God in Christ successfully searches out the lost
and sets in motion the hospitality of redemption.

Why was Zacchaeus especially loathed in
Jericho?

PRAYER: God, when I feel unloved and unwanted,
recall to my memory Zacchaeus, so that in his
story I will recognize how you discover my needs
and fulfill my deepest desires. Be welcome in my
heart and in my home. *Amen.*

"Wrapped It Up in a Piece of Cloth"
READ Luke 19:11–27

"Then the other came, saying, 'Lord, here
is your pound. I wrapped it up in a piece
of cloth, for I was afraid of you, because
you are a harsh man; you take what you
did not deposit, and reap what you did
not sow.'"

Luke 19:20–21

Faith risks failures in a life of obedience. The basic
sin for the Christian is not failure but disobedience.
Our failures rather than our sloth put us under the
divine judgment.

What, for you, is the key verse in the parable?

PRAYER: You have given me gifts beyond reason,
O God: capacity to love, strength to work, feelings
of compassion, knowledge of your ways. Help me
to use them in exchange with everyone I meet,
sharing and trading, giving and receiving. For
Jesus' sake. Amen.

"Glory in the Highest Heaven!"

READ Luke 19:28–40

"Blessed is the king
who comes in the name of the Lord!
Peace in heaven,
and glory in the highest heaven!"

Luke 19:38

As Jesus entered Jerusalem he acted out a parable of his lordship: the demonstrated rule of God exercised in peace and humility. No one ever had a king like that! Many responded—and still do—with exuberant praise.

Why did the Pharisees not join in the praise?

PRAYER: Dear Christ, ride into the center of my life and release every joyful instinct for celebrating your presence. The more deeply I experience your rule, the more deeply I am moved to praise you. Amen.

"He Wept Over It"

As he came near and saw the city, he wept
over it, saying, "If you, even you, had
only recognized on this day the things
that make for peace! But now they are
hidden from your eyes."

Luke 19:41–42

Jesus, surveying the holy city, and anticipating both rejection and crucifixion, does not respond, as we might expect, with seething anger, but in heartrending lament. He who knows us at our worst continues to love us. He does not reject us. And still he intercedes for us (Hebrews 7:25).

What are the things that "make for peace"?

PRAYER: God, forgive me for being unresponsive to your lordship and insensitive to your love. Deliver me from the ignorance that knows not the things that make for peace. *Amen.*

"House of Prayer . . . Den of Robbers"
READ Luke 19:45–48

.. and he said, "It is written,
 'My house shall be a house of prayer';
 but you have made it a den of robbers."
Luke 19:46

When human beings replace the intense, personal interchange between themselves and God that is prayer with commercial haggling over material possessions, arguing with each other over price instead of wrestling with God over eternal values, it's time for a thorough "spring cleaning."

Why did some seek to destroy Jesus?

PRAYER: Lord, renovate this "temple of your Holy Spirit" so that it will be a house of prayer. I need a good housecleaning from you to purge all the "buying and selling" that takes place in my heart. "Put a new and right spirit within me" (Psalm 51:10). Amen.

"From Heaven or of Human Origin?"
READ Luke 20:1–8

"Did the baptism of John come from
heaven, or was it of human origin?"
Luke 20:4

Everyone has to make a choice about Jesus: to admire and respect him as a fine man who said many exemplary things, in which case he is grist for discussion and argument; or to confess that he is God's Christ with authority to save and redeem, in which case we can only adore and obey him.

Why did Jesus decline to answer the question?

PRAYER: I see now, Jesus, that you aren't interested in my arguments and discussions; you are after my adoration and obedience. Help me to spend my time, not in sharpening arguments, but in perfecting praise. Amen.

"The Stone That the Builders Rejected"
READ Luke 20:9–18

> But he looked at them and said, "What
>   then does this text mean:
>   'The stone that the builders rejected
>   has become the cornerstone'?"

Luke 20:17

No one gets rid of Jesus by rejecting him; he is an unavoidable presence in everyone's life. That presence can be an irritant (if we insist, proudly and selfishly, on living for ourselves) or it can be glorious good news, as we let him shape our lives by his lordship.

Which psalm does Jesus quote from?

PRAYER: When I insist on living as if you don't exist, Jesus, you are a stumbling block to me; but when I receive you in faith as my Savior, what a magnificent cornerstone you are to this temple that is my body. *Amen.*

"In Order to Trap Him"
READ Luke 20:19–26

So they watched him and sent spies who
pretended to be honest, in order to trap
him by what he said, so as to hand him
over to the jurisdiction and authority of
the governor.

Luke 20:20

Jesus will not be drawn into our petty disputes.
He sends us back to our responsibilities—to be
good citizens and to serve God faithfully with our
whole heart and mind and strength. We misunderstand Jesus completely if we suppose that he is
going to be party to our squabbles.

What belongs to "Caesar"?

PRAYER: How simple you make things, Jesus. Your
lordship puts everything in its place: my obligations in this world are maintained, but not at the
expense of giving you my total loyalty and worship. Amen.

"God Not of the Dead, but of the Living"
READ Luke 20:27–40

"Now he is God not of the dead, but of the
living; for to him all of them are alive."

Luke 20:38

The mind of humankind invents puzzles to which
there seem to be no solutions. But that is because
we "know neither the scriptures nor the power of
God" (Matthew 22:29). God is not an idea we use
to figure out hard questions. He is our living
Lord, actively creating and redeeming this world.

Why was the Sadducees' question silly?

PRAYER: I talk about you, Lord, when I should be
talking to you. I lose touch with the living quality
of your presence and get into long-winded discussions about your reputation. Bring me back to
a fresh, personal relationship in Jesus Christ. Amen.

"In the Book of Psalms"

READ Luke 20:41–44

"For David himself says in the book of Psalms,
'The Lord said to my Lord,
"Sit at my right hand,
until I make your enemies your
footstool." ' "

Luke 20:42–43

Unlike his opponents, Jesus did not quote scripture to prove a point or win an argument; he lived it. Immersed in its language, and particularly that of the psalms, he fulfilled it in all his words and deeds.

From which psalm does Jesus quote?

PRAYER: Lord God, I want to learn to read scripture your way; using its vocabulary to speak my prayers; making its story the structure for my life; realizing its truths in my daily round, after the manner and in the power of Jesus Christ. *Amen.*

"Long Prayers"

READ Luke 20:45–47

"They devour widows' houses and for the
sake of appearance say long prayers. They
will receive the greater condemnation."

Luke 20:47

As experts in religion, the scribes were looked up
to. But their knowledge was all in their heads—in
their hearts they remained selfish and proud. They
used "long prayers" as a smoke screen to camou
flage their sordid ambition.

Do you know anyone like the scribes?

PRAYER: Train me, God, to be wary of people who
advertise their righteousness, and to remember
that "long prayers" are no substitute for obedient
love. Keep my vision fixed on you. *Amen.*

"A Poor Widow"

READ Luke 21:1–4

He looked up and saw rich people putting
their gifts into the treasury; he also saw a
poor widow put in two small copper
coins.

Luke 21:1–2

Jesus focused his blazing insight on the common-
place contrast between the contributions of the
rich and the offerings of the poor, and made an
unforgettable drama of it: "[mortals] look on the
appearance, but the LORD looks on the heart"
(1 Samuel 16:7).

What do you learn about your own offerings
from this?

PRAYER: "We give Thee but Thine own, Whate'er
the gift may be: All that we have is Thine alone, A
trust, O Lord, from Thee" (William Walsham
How, "We Give Thee but Thine Own"). *Amen.*

"Beware"

READ Luke 21:5–9

And he said, "Beware that you are not led
astray; for many will come in my name
and say 'I am he!' and 'The time is near!'
Do not go after them."

Luke 21:8

Patient endurance is not the same as lazy sleepiness. Jesus tells us not to be alarmed, but that doesn't mean that we are permitted to be complacent. Alertness is commanded. We live in a world full of claims and counterclaims; we must distinguish between them and hold fast to what Christ says.

What false reports do you disbelieve?

PRAYER: When I decided to believe in you, Jesus, I also decided not to believe in a lot of other people. Help me to alertly discriminate between your saving word and the false promises of others. Amen.

"By Your Endurance"

READ Luke 21:10–19

"By your endurance you will gain your
  souls."

Luke 21:19

It is easy enough to become distracted, alarmed,
and anxious as we live in a chaotic world threat-
ened by disaster and ruin. But Jesus anticipates
our panic and counsels patient endurance. The
end is in his hands, not in the hands of politicians
or generals.

How does a Christian develop endurance?

PRAYER: How easily I am thrown off balance by
the bad news that comes through headlines and
gossip—as if anything on this earth could alter
your final victory. Deepen my trust in your sure
ways and your majestic rule. Amen.

"Days of Vengeance"

READ Luke 21:20–24

> "Then those in Judea must flee to the
> mountains, and those inside the city
> must leave it, and those out in the
> country must not enter it; for these are
> days of vengeance, as a fulfillment of all
> that is written."

Luke 21:21–22

"The times of the Gentiles" have to do with humanity living with the consequences of its own evil. But what human beings do to one another is not "the end." However terrible it is, our Lord provides the means for his people to be faithful to him through it.

What "great distress" do you observe in history?

PRAYER: "Who trusts in God, a strong abode in heaven and earth possesses, who looks in love to Christ above, no fear his heart oppresses. In Thee alone, dear Lord, we own sweet hope and consolation; our shield from foes, our balm for woes, our great and sure salvation" (Joachim Magdeburg, "Who Trusts in God, a Strong Abode"). *Amen.*

"Raise Your Heads"

READ Luke 21:25–28

"Now when these things begin to take
   place, stand up and raise your heads,
   because your redemption is drawing
   near."

Luke 21:28

Jesus says three things about the end: one, he will
return (that gives us hope); two, no mortal knows
the date (that saves us from all anxious curiosity);
three, watch. We must concentrate all our energy
on faithfully following a living Christ, not com-
piling a timetable for him.

How do you prepare for our Lord's coming
again?

PRAYER: What a mistake it would be for me to get
so interested in when you return that I quit preparing for your return. At your return, Jesus, I
want to be found at my job of being your disciple,
not off on the sidelines talking about it. *Amen.*

"Look at the Fig Tree"

READ Luke 21:29–33

Then he told them a parable: "Look at the
fig tree and all the trees; as soon as they
sprout leaves you can see for yourselves
and know that summer is already near."

Luke 21:29–30

Just as the world of nature is generous with signs
of changing seasons, so the world of redemption
is full of signs. Every report of disorder, each head
line of dismay is evidence that this world is not our
home and that the kingdom of God is just across
the threshold. Strange people, these Christians,
whose hope increases when the world seems to
be disintegrating?

What sign of hope can you glean from the disorder in today's world?

PRAYER: O God, I will not be bowed down or dis-
heartened by the tired reports of sin and destruc-
tion. I will take your words to heart and lift my
head in hope, confident that the day of redemption is nearer than it has ever been before. Amen.

JUNE 1

"Be Alert at All Times"
READ Luke 21:34–38

"Be alert at all times, praying that you may
have the strength to escape all these
things that will take place, and to stand
before the Son of Man."

Luke 21:36

The accumulation of days and years can become a
sluggish weight from which we attempt escape,
or it can be a rich tradition to use as background
while we live alertly and watchfully for God's
coming to us in Jesus Christ.

How do you cultivate watchfulness?

PRAYER: "Now to him who by the power at work
within us is able to accomplish abundantly far
more than all we can ask or imagine, to him be
glory in the church and in Christ Jesus to all generations, forever and ever" (Ephesians 3:20–21).
Amen.

"Judas Called Iscariot"

READ Luke 22:1–6

Then Satan entered into Judas called
Iscariot, who was one of the twelve; he
went away and conferred with the chief
priests and officers of the temple police
about how he might betray him to them.

Luke 22:3–4

The gospel invites us to give ourselves and what
we have to our Lord that he may save us. But
many, like Judas, shrewdly and selfishly, are so intent on getting whatever they can from him that
they never hear the invitation. Jesus is a Lord to be
served, not an "opportunity" for turning a quick
profit.

What did Judas hope to gain from his betrayal?

PRAYER: Every time, O God, that I slip into the old
ways of calculating how I can advance my interests
by being known as your disciple, remind me that
that was Judas's way, and it amounts to a horrible
betrayal of your Son. Amen.

"A Large Room Upstairs"
READ Luke 22:7–13

"He will show you a large room upstairs,
  already furnished. Make preparations for
  us there."

Luke 22:12

The disciples thought they were doing the most mundane of tasks, following a man with a water jar and getting a room ready for a feast. In fact, they were setting the scene for the institution of the Lord's Supper. We never know how God will use our everyday acts of obedience. What we suppose is trivial may be preliminary to a mighty act of salvation.

Do you think the man with the water jar was conscious of the part he played in the drama?

PRAYER: Whatever I do today, Lord, whether I am alone reading a book or visiting with friends, lazily indulging in some leisure or busily getting something done, "whether [I] eat or drink" (1 Corinthians 10:31), by your grace I will do it to your glory, through Jesus Christ. *Amen.*

"This Is My Body"

READ Luke 22:14–23

Then he took a loaf of bread, and when
he had given thanks, he broke it and
gave it to them, saying, "This is my
body, which is given for you. Do this
in remembrance of me."

Luke 22:19

By Jesus' command the "last supper" became the
"Lord's Supper"—a continuous sign by which
Christians in faith receive the life of Christ and
keep alive the promise of the final "supper of the
Lamb" in heaven.

Why does the Lord's Supper continue to be so
important for Christians?

PRAYER: "Thy body, broken for my sake, My bread
from heaven shall be; Thy testamental cup I take,
And thus remember Thee. Remember Thee, and
all Thy pains, And all Thy love to me: Yea, while a
breath, a pulse remains Will I remember Thee"
(James Montgomery, "According to Thy Gracious
Word," in The Hymnbook, p. 444). Amen.

"Sit on Thrones"

READ Luke 22:24–30

> "You are those who have stood by me in
> my trials; and I confer on you, just as my
> Father has conferred on me, a kingdom,
> so that you may eat and drink at my
> table in my kingdom, and you will sit
> on thrones judging the twelve tribes of
> Israel."
>
> Luke 22:28–30

The question in the disciples' hearts is, And what are we going to get out of it? They want some guarantee that "grace" pays off. Instead of sharply rebuking them for immaturity, Jesus graciously meets them on their level and assures them that life in the kingdom of God will be resplendent with reward.

How does your hope of future benefits affect your present discipleship?

PRAYER: O God, allay all the anxieties I have about the future, so that I may simply accept the great things you have for me, confident that what no eye has seen, nor ear heard, nor the human heart conceived, you have prepared for those who love you (1 Corinthians 2:9). *Amen.*

"I Have Prayed for You"

READ Luke 22:31–34

"Simon, Simon, listen! Satan has demanded
to sift all of you like wheat, but I have
prayed for you that your own faith may
not fail; and you, when once you have
turned back, strengthen your brothers."

Luke 22:31–32

Our denials are no surprise to our Lord, even if
they are to us. He anticipates them and provides
for our restoration. His prayers for us are foundation stones for a life built, not on our strength,
but on his forgiveness.

Have you ever thought you were strong in an
area where temptation exposed a weakness you
didn't know was there?

PRAYER: I am learning, Jesus, not to rely on my
own boastful resolutions, but rather to trust your
grace, which invades my weakness with strength
and my failures with redemption. Amen.

"It Is Enough"

READ Luke 22:35–38

They said, "Lord, look, here are two
swords." He replied, "It is enough."

Luke 22:38

Patiently and persistently Jesus taught his disciples
to be prepared for the crucifixion and resurrection. They had learned the adequacy of grace in
the everyday routines of discipleship; now they
would experience it in the crisis of crucifixion
and resurrection.

What were the two swords for?

PRAYER: I am always trying to separate your way
from my way, Lord. I think that your life was special and mine is ordinary. Help me to realize that
every decision you made throws illumination on
what I must decide in the practical affairs of my
discipleship, so that as I follow your ways, I also
may lack nothing. *Amen.*

JUNE 8

"Father"

READ Luke 22:39–46

> "Father, if you are willing, remove this cup
> from me; yet, not my will but yours be
> done."

Luke 22:42

Jesus' prayer in Gethsemane shows him facing the deepest sorrow and suffering—and finding in the Father's will the strength and love to do whatever is necessary for our salvation.

How is this similar to Jesus' time of temptation in the wilderness (see Luke 4:1–13)?

PRAYER: What a contrast between the sleeping disciples and the praying Christ! God, teach me to pray like my Lord: to put your will above my own and to persevere until I have the strength and will to face any demands you make. *Amen.*

"Swords and Clubs"
READ Luke 22:47–53

Then Jesus said to [them], "Have you come
out with swords and clubs as if I were a
bandit?"

Luke 22:52

For a moment it looked as if the money that could
buy a betrayal and the swords and clubs that
could make an arrest were ascendant. But Jesus
did not waver—in the melee of brandished clubs
and traitorous embrace, his response (how characteristic!) was to heal the servant with the sev-
ered ear.

Why were the soldiers so heavily armed?

PRAYER: Lord, how foolish, how futile, to try to
avoid your love. All that scheming and plotting!
All that violence! I want to expend what energy I
have in following and serving you. Amen.

"Went Out and Wept Bitterly"
READ Luke 22:54–62

The Lord turned and looked at Peter. Then
Peter remembered the word of the Lord,
how he had said to him, "Before the cock
crows today, you will deny me three
times." And he went out and wept
bitterly.

Luke 22:61–62

Peter is a model for Christians, not because he
never sinned—he did, most grievously—but because he faced his sin and felt anguished remorse.
His "godly sorrow" opened his heart to grace and
forgiveness.

Have you ever done anything comparable to
Peter's denial?

PRAYER: I review the past few days and remember
the times I have failed to bear witness to you, O
Christ. Forgive me, and build a holy boldness in
me that is proud to acknowledge your lordship.
Amen.

"Began to Mock Him"
READ Luke 22:63–65

Now the men who were holding Jesus
began to mock him and beat him; they
also blindfolded him and kept asking him,
"Prophesy! Who is it that struck you?"
Luke 22:63–64

Mortals, with no other reason to reject God than that they want to be gods themselves, erupt in furious and blasphemous violence against the Christ. It was as if the soldiers were unconscious agents for all the hostility of all the ages against God's rule and love.

Do you think the soldiers had any idea of Jesus' real identity?

PRAYER: God, when I'm with the wrong crowd I get involved in their mockeries. You come to me with your very best, but I miss seeing it—I make fun of what you bring in my life to be adored. Purify my perceptions so that I may see clearly what you are doing and in whom you are working, so that I may worship and follow, in Jesus' name. *Amen.*

"Are You, Then, the Son of God?"

READ Luke 22:66–71

All of them asked, "Are you, then, the Son of God?" He said to them, "You say that I am."

Luke 22:70

It was not Jesus who was on trial that day, but the chief priests and scribes. When human beings make decisions against Christ, they do not put him out of office, they put themselves out of harmony with his will. Jesus did not become Lord by a majority election, and he cannot be banished from his throne by our votes.

What were the charges against Jesus?

PRAYER: Help me, O God, to make my decisions about you based on what you have revealed yourself to be in Jesus, not on what men and women say about you. *Amen.*

JUNE 13

"Pilate"

READ Luke 23:1–5

Then the assembly rose as a body and
brought Jesus before Pilate.

Luke 23:1

Jesus, sure of his rule and destiny, offered neither defense nor explanation to Pilate, a man who, though he administered the massive power of Rome, had no power for good or ill over the Christ of God.

Do you think that Pilate took Jesus seriously?

PRAYER: God, prevent me from being easily impressed with the Pilates of this world, the ones who command worldly power. Create in me a poise that confidently waits for you to work your sure purpose in Jesus Christ. Amen.

"Herod"

READ Luke 23:6–12

When Herod saw Jesus, he was very glad,
   for he had been wanting to see him for a
   long time, because he had heard about
   him and was hoping to see him perform
   some sign.

Luke 23:8

Herod, satiated and bored, wanted Jesus to divert
him with a miracle. The things of God were no
more, for him, than materials for a nightclub act.
The Herodian motive is frequently discernible,
still, in our hearts: we want God to excite, divert,
or stimulate us. And if he will not do it when we
snap our fingers, we impatiently seek out another
form of entertainment.

Why did Herod and Pilate become friends?

PRAYER: Almighty God, do I do that? Do I demand
daily diversions from your Holy Spirit? Lead me
beneath the surface sensations of religion into the
deeper waters of faithful love and persevering
prayer. For Jesus' sake. *Amen.*

"Have Not Found This Man Guilty"

READ Luke 23:13–17

Pilate then called together the chief priests,
the leaders, and the people, and said to
them, "You brought me this man as one
who was perverting the people; and here
I have examined him in your presence
and have not found this man guilty of
any of your charges against him."

Luke 23:13–14

In a world seething with proud human beings
who would provoke us to insurrection and clever
ones who would deceive us by imposture, it is
important that Jesus be tested against those possibilities. Pilate and Herod conducted just such an
examination and found no evidence of guilt.

What were the charges against Jesus?

PRAYER: "Ah, holy Jesus, how hast Thou offended, That man to judge Thee hath in hate pretended? By foes derided, by Thine own rejected,
O most afflicted!" (Johann Heermann, "Ah, Holy
Jesus, How Hast Thou Offended," in *The Hymnbook*,
p. 191). *Amen.*

JUNE 16

"Barabbas"

READ Luke 23:18–25

Then they all shouted out together, "Away
with this fellow! Release Barabbas for us!"
Luke 23:18

We are all like Barabbas: persons condemned to
death for our own sins and then wondrously and
unexpectedly released as the innocent Christ is
put in our place to die for us.

How do you suppose Barabbas felt at his release?

PRAYER: "Not the labors of my hands Can fulfill
Thy law's demands; Could my zeal no respite
know, Could my tears forever flow, All for sin
could not atone; Thou must save, and Thou alone"
(Augustus M. Toplady, "Rock of Ages, Cleft for
Me"). Amen.

JUNE 17

"Simon of Cyrene"
READ Luke 23:26–31

As they led him away, they seized a man,
Simon of Cyrene, who was coming from
the country, and they laid the cross on
him, and made him carry it behind Jesus.
Luke 23:26

Simon, carrying the cross for Jesus, and the women
bewailing the injustice of his condemnation, par-
ticipated in our Lord's rejection and shared his
suffering. Their example—embracing (not avoiding) the person in pain and sharing (not denying)
the cruelties of condemnation—has permanently
influenced the Christian style of life.

Whose cross can you bear? Whose pain can
you lament?

PRAYER: I thank you, Lord, for those who have
helped to bear my burdens, who have visited me
when I was sick and put up with me when I was
depressed, who have shared my tears and your
comfort. Amen.

"Save Yourself!"

READ Luke 23:32–38

> The soldiers also mocked him, coming up
> and offering him sour wine, and saying,
> "If you are the King of the Jews, save
> yourself!"

Luke 23:36–37

The soldiers spoke better than they knew. When they mocked "the King of the Jews" they supposed they were only indulging their whimsy; in fact, they were announcing the ruler of creation: "The LORD is king, he is robed in majesty" (Psalm 93:1).

Why didn't Jesus save himself?

PRAYER: What those Roman soldiers did in jest, O Christ, let me do in awed reverence: pay full homage to you as ruler of all creation, "King of Kings and Lord of Lords" (Revelations 19:16). Amen.

"Today You Will Be with Me in Paradise"
READ Luke 23:39–43

Then he said, "Jesus, remember me when
you come into your kingdom." He
replied, "Truly I tell you, today you will
be with me in Paradise."

Luke 23:42–43

The clearest words spoken by our Lord about life
after death were addressed to a criminal. Remembering that, we cannot suppose that eternal life is
the natural conclusion to our goodness. It is initiated from the other direction. It is not what we
strive toward and achieve; it is what God creates
and provides as a gift.

What do you know about Paradise?

PRAYER: Lord Jesus, thank you for your promise:
not a cheap paradise constructed out of my wish-fulfillment fantasies, but an eternity of simply
being with you. *Amen.*

JUNE 20

"Father, into Your Hands"
READ Luke 23:44–49

Then Jesus, crying with a loud voice, said,
"Father, into your hands I commend
my spirit." Having said this, he breathed
his last.

Luke 23:46

The death of Jesus threw the world into darkness;
the anguished prayer and the torn temple curtain
marked the end of an era. But this end was also a
beginning, a beginning marked by the perceptive
centurion's exclamation, "Certainly this man was
innocent" (v. 47).

What led the centurion to praise God?

PRAYER: "What thou, my Lord, hast suffered Was
all for sinners' gain: Mine, mine was the trans-
gression, But Thine the deadly pain. Lo, here I fall,
my Saviour! 'Tis I deserve Thy place; Look on me
with Thy favor, Vouchsafe to me Thy grace"
(Bernard of Clairvaux, "O Sacred Head, Now
Wounded"). Amen.

"A Rock-Hewn Tomb"
READ Luke 23:50–56

Then he took it down, wrapped it in a
linen cloth, and laid it in a rock-hewn
tomb where no one had ever been laid.

Luke 23:53

The burial of Jesus is a link between the worst that human beings could do to God's Son (crucify him) and the best that they could do (devotedly and compassionately lay him in a tomb). They poured out first their hate, then their love, on Jesus. Now, what would God do?

What motivated Joseph to this act of kindness?

PRAYER: "What language shall I borrow To thank Thee, dearest Friend, For this Thy dying sorrow, Thy pity without end? O make me Thine forever; And should I fainting be, Lord, let me never, never Outlive my love to Thee" (Bernard of Clairvaux, "O Sacred Head, Now Wounded"). *Amen.*

JUNE 22

"Perplexed"
READ Luke 24:1–12

While they were perplexed about this,
suddenly two men in dazzling clothes
stood beside them.

Luke 24:4

The women expected to deal with the great human realities of death and the tomb. They were stunned to find that both had already been dealt with! From that moment on, they were free to acknowledge the great new divine reality of resurrection.

Why is the resurrection important to you?

PRAYER: Father, you know how anxiously, sorrowfully, and grimly I approach death. I need, again, the full story of my risen Lord. "Let him easter in us, be a dayspring to the dimness of us, be a crimson-crested east" (Gerard Manley Hopkins, "The Wreck of the Deutschland," *Poems and Prose of G. M. Hopkins* [Baltimore: Penguin Books, 1953], p. 24). *Amen.*

"Looking Sad"

READ Luke 24:13–20

And he said to them, "What are you
discussing with each other while you
walk along?" They stood still, looking sad.

Luke 24:17

The resurrection is God's great surprise. Amazement was a natural reaction. No one expected it; no one was prepared for it. By now, though, Christians know that resurrection is God's most characteristic action.

Why were the two apostles so slow to catch on?

PRAYER: "'Tis the spring of souls today: Christ hath burst His prison, And from three days' sleep in death As a sun hath risen; All the winter of our sins, Long and dark, is flying From His light, to whom we give Laud and praise undying" (John of Damascus, "Come, Ye Faithful, Raise the Strain"). *Amen.*

JUNE 24

"But We Had Hoped"
READ Luke 24:21–25

"But we had hoped that he was the one to
redeem Israel. Yes, and besides all this, it
is now the third day since these things
took place."

Luke 24:21

They had hoped; were they still hoping? Yes, they
were still hoping. Hope that is worth its salt hopes
when things no longer look hopeful. Hope is a
sturdy virtue and doesn't collapse under despair-
ing opinion polls.

Which is the hardest for you—faith, hope, or
love?

PRAYER: After three days, O God, I don't know if I
would have still been hoping. Don't let blank days
on the calendar diminish my hope; nurture my
hope in prayer and promise, in Jesus' name. *Amen.*

JUNE 25

"Beginning with Moses"
READ Luke 24:26–27

Then beginning with Moses and all the
    prophets, he interpreted to them the
    things about himself in all the scriptures.
                                        Luke 24:27

The resurrection was not something that God
thought up at the last minute after everything else
had failed. It was his plan from the beginning. For
centuries, God, in interaction with his people,
had developed the means of grace and the theme
of salvation, to which the resurrection was climax
and conclusion.

What scriptures would Jesus have been sure to
mention?

PRAYER: Lord Jesus Christ, as I read scripture, interpret to me the age-old rootage of your salvation
in the soil of your people, and the wide sweep of
your purposes developed in your prophets, all of
which came to fulfillment in you. *Amen.*

"They Recognized Him"

READ Luke 24:28–32

Then their eyes were opened, and they
recognized him; and he vanished from
their sight.

Luke 24:31

Similar instances of recognition continue in the
Christian community. believers gather together to
study scripture and break bread; the risen Lord
meets with them to inspire and to interpret.

With whom do you meet for fellowship and
learning?

PRAYER: Open my mind to understand all that the
scriptures say about you, dear Lord. Warm my
heart to respond to all that you promise and fulfill. *Amen.*

JUNE 27

"They Told What Had Happened"
READ Luke 24:33–35

Then they told what had happened on the
road, and how he had been made known
to them in the breaking of the bread.

Luke 24:35

The resurrection is an experience to be shared and
news to be proclaimed. The single most important thing Christians have to say to one another is
that Christ is alive among us.

Who has recently told you of something related
to the risen Christ?

PRAYER: Lord Christ, open up a conversation for
me today in which I can talk of what is most important to me, your risen presence in my life, so
that at least one additional person may know that
you are risen indeed. *Amen.*

"Startled and Terrified"
READ Luke 24:36–44

They were startled and terrified, and
thought that they were seeing a ghost.

Luke 24:37

The resurrection, the most extraordinary thing
that ever happened, enters into the most ordinary
routines. It is not to be confused with the weird-
ness of the occult or the fantasies of superstition.
To deny the risen Lord participation in our common round of life is as great an act of disbelief as
to refuse belief in his resurrection at all.

What did Jesus' eating demonstrate?

PRAYER: Even in the glorious moments of your
resurrection appearances, Lord Jesus, you made it
plain that you are in touch with the world I live
in, a world of physical needs and emotional stress.
In gratitude I receive your risen presence in this
day's living. *Amen.*

"Power from on High"

READ Luke 24:45–49

"And see, I am sending upon you what my
Father promised; so stay here in the city
until you have been clothed with power
from on high."

Luke 24:49

The disciples were to be more than observers of the
marvels of the resurrection; they were to be participants in it, convinced and credible witnesses to
the risen Christ. They were to become powerful
and persistent confederates in the way of salvation.

What was the "power from on high" they were
to receive?

PRAYER: Empower me to live, dear God, all that I
have seen and heard in Jesus. I wait for the en-
abling gift of your Holy Spirit to bring all your
promises to fulfillment in me. *Amen.*

"Great Joy"

READ Luke 24:50–53

And they worshiped him, and returned to
Jerusalem with great joy; and they were
continually in the temple blessing God.
Luke 24:52–53

The exchange of a visible Savior, demonstrating
God's loving redemption, for an invisible Lord,
ruling in eternal mercy and might, took place in
an atmosphere of great joy. There were no tears at
this parting—it was the happiest of transitions.

What are the two ways in which "bless" is used
here?

PRAYER: "The Lord ascendeth up on high, The
Lord hath triumphed gloriously, In power and
might excelling; The grave and hell are captive
led, Lo! He returns, our glorious Head, To His
eternal dwelling" (Arthur T. Russell, "The Lord
Ascendeth Up on High"). *Amen.*

"All That Jesus Did and Taught"
READ *Acts* 1:1–2

> In the first book, Theophilus, I wrote about
> all that Jesus did and taught from the
> beginning until the day when he was
> taken up to heaven, after giving
> instructions through the Holy Spirit to
> the apostles whom he had chosen.
>
> *Acts* 1:1–2

The Acts of the Apostles is the second volume of Luke's two-volume work. The Gospel of Luke covers the ministry of Jesus; Acts is the story of the early church. What Jesus "did and taught from the beginning" is now seen as it has consequence in the world.

This is St. Luke's second volume. What stands out for you as characteristic of his first volume, the Gospel?

PRAYER: "Blessed Lord, who has caused all holy scriptures to be written for our learning: Grant that we may in such wise hear them, read, mark, learn, and inwardly digest them, that by patience, and comfort of Thy Holy Word, we may embrace and ever hold fast the blessed hope of everlasting life, which Thou has given us in our Saviour Jesus Christ" (*Book of Common Worship*). *Amen.*

JULY 2

"Many Convincing Proofs"

READ Acts 1:3

> After his suffering he presented himself
> alive to them by many convincing
> proofs, appearing to them during forty
> days and speaking about the kingdom
> of God.
>
> Acts 1:3

The forty days of testing and examination by the
enemy at the beginning of Jesus' ministry (Luke
4:1–13) is now matched by a similar forty days
of examination at its conclusion, but this time by
his friends. The ministry of Jesus is no unverified
rumor; it is a thoroughly examined and tested
reality.

What convinces you that Jesus is who he said
he was, and your Lord?

PRAYER: Thank you, dear Lord, for so generously
providing the "many proofs" that encourage re-
liance on your word and trust in your acts. Sustain
me against doubts. In Jesus' name. Amen.

"Wait There for the Promise"

READ *Acts* 1:4–5

While staying with them, he ordered them
not to leave Jerusalem, but to wait there for
the promise of the Father. "This," he said,
"is what you have heard from me. . . ."

Acts 1:4

The sequel to Jesus' ministry is the ministry of the
Holy Spirit. The first is outward and historical; the
second is inward and personal. All that God did
publicly in Jesus he now promises to do personally
in the believer.

What is "the promise of the Father"?

PRAYER: I wait for your promise, O God. Everything that you have done in Jesus, do now in me.
I want my life to be the "holy land" in which you
speak your word and demonstrate your ministry.
Amen.

"You Will Receive Power"

READ Acts 1:6–8

"But you will receive power when the
   Holy Spirit has come upon you; and you
   will be my witnesses in Jerusalem, in all
   Judea and Samaria, and to the ends of
   the earth."

Acts 1:8

The Christian life is not a privileged look into the
future, but an adequacy to live in the present. The
Holy Spirit draws us away from gossiping about
God, or imagining utopias, and into a day-by-day
witness in real towns and cities.

What is the power of the Holy Spirit for?

PRAYER: "O Spirit of the living God, In all Thy
plenitude of grace, Where'er the foot of man hath
trod, Descend on our apostate race. Baptize the
nations; far and nigh The triumphs of the cross
record; the name of Jesus glorify, Till every kindred
call Him Lord" (James Montgomery, "O Spirit of
the Living God"). Amen.

"He Was Lifted Up"
READ Acts 1:9–11

When he had said this, as they were
watching, he was lifted up, and a cloud
took him out of their sight.

Acts 1:9

Jesus became absent to the sight of a few so that
he could be present to all in the Holy Spirit. He
now, in the familiar words of the Apostles' Creed,
"sitteth on the right hand of God the Father
Almighty, from thence He shall come to judge the
quick and the dead."

What do you think your feelings would have
been if you had been physically present at the as-
cension?

PRAYER: Lord, I don't want to be among those
who stand "gazing into heaven" reminiscing over
the past, no matter how glorious. Your departures
are not an impoverishment but a plenitude. Help
me to respond in expectation, not retreat in regret.
Amen.

"Devoting Themselves to Prayer"
READ Acts 1:12–14

All these were constantly devoting
themselves to prayer, together with
certain women, including Mary the
mother of Jesus, as well as his brothers.

Acts 1:14

The disciples, living under their Lord's command
to wait for the promise, did not desultorily "kill
time" nervously hoping that something would
turn up. Instead, they creatively gave themselves
to the intensities of prayer.

What is your attitude when you have to wait?

PRAYER: Lord, as I wait for the fulfillment of your
promises, help me to do it with grace, not chafing
at delays, but devotedly finding your mind in
Christ. *Amen.*

JULY 7

"Concerning Judas"
READ *Acts* 1:15–20

"Friends, the scripture had to be fulfilled,
    which the Holy Spirit through David
    foretold concerning Judas, who became
    a guide for those who arrested Jesus—
    for he was numbered among us and was
    allotted his share in this ministry."

Acts 1:16–17

The way the disciples dealt with the memory of
Judas is instructive. His sin was criminal in the
extreme, yet they neither suppressed nor sensa-
tionalized it; they simply set it in the context of
scripture and found guidance to continue in
obedience.

Which psalms does Peter quote?

PRAYER: More than ever, Father, I am determined
to be at home in your scriptures, so that nothing
other people can do will throw me off the track of
following you. I will see everything, even those
things that look absolutely disastrous to me, in the
context of your providence, which steadily moves
to redemption. In Jesus' name. *Amen.*

JULY 8

"One of These"

READ *Acts 1:21–22*

". . . one of these must become a witness
with us to his resurrection."

Acts 1:22b

In the middle of the prayer meeting, there was a
brief adjournment for committee work! While
they were waiting for God to fulfill his promise,
the disciples made sure that they had done all they
could to fulfill their responsibilities.

What is the most interesting thing you do in
the church?

PRAYER: It is easy for me to forget, O God, that
you work through the most mundane processes
to achieve your will. Prevent me from ever treating with contempt the behind-the-scenes labors
and less-than-glamorous routines that are also a
part of your church. *Amen.*

JULY 9

"Matthias"

READ *Acts* 1:23–26

So they proposed two, Joseph called
Barsabbas, who was also known as
Justus, and Matthias.

Acts 1:23

Leadership is essential, but prominence is not. The apostles were sensitive to the needs of ministry but indifferent to matters of publicity. Matthias, as Judas's replacement, is not heard from again: his apostolic work of witness to the resurrection was done quietly and modestly, but no less effectively than the work of those about whom we hear more.

What contrasts do you see between Judas and Matthias?

PRAYER: I give thanks, dear Father, for that great majority in the Christian community who work faithfully and devotedly behind the scenes, never raising their voices and never flagging in their devotion, as witnesses to your resurrection. *Amen.*

"All Together in One Place"

READ Acts 2:1

When the day of Pentecost had come, they
were all together in one place.

Acts 2:1

We do not get God's gifts by entering into fierce
competition with one another and vying for pref-
erential treatment, but by coming "together in
one place." Our coming together is the raw material God uses to create a community of the Spirit
in which diversities complement and differences
harmonize.

Compare this with Acts 1:14.

PRAYER: Holy Spirit, lower barriers of defensive-
ness between me and my neighbors; eliminate
suspicion that separates me from other Christians,
include me in the company of those you are making into a whole and harmonious church. *Amen.*

"Suddenly from Heaven"

READ *Acts* 2:2–4

And suddenly from heaven there came a
   sound like the rush of a violent wind,
   and it filled the entire house where they
   were sitting.

Acts 2:2

The Holy Spirit descends; and the church begins.
The promise for which the apostles were waiting
is fulfilled, but not secretly nor privately—it is
public and it is wonderful. The sights and sounds
of Pentecost are unavoidable evidence that God is
active among his people.

What do the "tongues of fire" mean here?

PRAYER: "Come, Holy Ghost, our souls inspire,
and lighten with celestial fire: Thou the anointing
Spirit art, who dost Thy sevenfold gifts impart.
Praise to Thy eternal merit, Father, Son and Holy
Spirit" (ancient hymn). *Amen.*

"In Our Own Native Language"

READ *Acts 2:5–11*

"And how is it that we hear, each of us, in
our own native language?"

Acts 2:8

Pentecost is Babel reversed. At Babel an original
unity was turned into confusion; at Pentecost the
confusion is sorted out into a language of proclamation and praise. A miracle of hearing takes place
and mortals hear, in a way they can understand,
"God's mighty deeds" (Acts 2:11).

How many nationalities are named?

PRAYER: God, I talk too much and listen not
enough. Give me the pentecostal gift of ears—the
ability to hear your mighty works proclaimed in
my own language. *Amen.*

JULY 13

"Amazed and Perplexed"
READ Acts 2:12–13

All were amazed and perplexed, saying to
one another, "What does this mean?"

Acts 2:12

The world, confronted with evidence of the Holy
Spirit's activities, divides into two groups: the
mockers ("They are filled with new wine") and the
inquirers ("What does this mean?"). Faced with
the wonders of God, we can either dismiss them
in derision or inquire after them in humility.

Do you ever make fun of things you don't
understand?

PRAYER: Almighty God, I don't want to reduce
the world to the dimensions of my mind just so I
can understand it. Rather, enlarge my faith so I can
comprehend and share the mighty works of God
to which I hear others giving witness. *Amen.*

"I Will Pour Out My Spirit"

READ *Acts* 2:14–21

> " 'In the last days it will be, God declares,
> that I will pour out my Spirit upon all
>   flesh,
> and your sons and your daughters shall
>   prophesy,
> and your young men shall see visions,
> and your old men shall dream dreams.' "

Acts 2:17

Peter begins his great Pentecost sermon with an explanation: the people who are telling the wonders of God are moved to do so by the Holy Spirit, the invisible cause of all witness and praise. But if invisible, the Spirit is not obscure but has been plainly talked about by Joel, to name only one of the prophets.

What are the results of the Spirit's coming, according to Joel?

PRAYER: Praise your name, O God! Your Spirit descends upon your people, and your promises come to life! Pour out your Spirit upon me and make great praises spring from my heart, for Jesus' sake. *Amen.*

JULY 15

"But God Raised Him Up"

"But God raised him up, having freed him
from death, because it was impossible
for him to be held in its power."

Acts 2:24

Peter continues his Pentecost sermon by review-
ing what happened to Jesus: in summary, human
beings killed him and God raised him. He is the
center for the worst that humankind can do and
the best that God does—and God's best is the final
word.

Find three things that Peter says about Jesus.

PRAYER: Father, help me to grasp everything that
you want to tell me in Jesus. There is so much to
reveal in his words and acts, and I don't want to
miss any of it. I offer my prayer in his strong
name. *Amen.*

JULY 16

"Know with Certainty"
READ *Acts* 2:29–36

"Therefore let the entire house of Israel
know with certainty that God has made
him both Lord and Messiah, this Jesus
whom you crucified."

Acts 2:36

Peter's choice of words—"confidently" (v. 29)
and "certainty" (v. 36)—shows his mood. He has
never stood on more solid ground. Eyewitnesses
and scriptural witnesses have converged at a single
point: Jesus is God's Christ. The resurrection is the
evidence.

What scriptures does Peter quote?

PRAYER: O God in Christ, sharpen my perceptions
of your works; intensify my responses to your
ways; make firm the foundations of my faith, so
that my witness may be clear and my obedience
bold. Amen.

"The Promise Is for You"
READ *Acts* 2:37–39

> "For the promise is for you, for your
> children, and for all who are far away,
> everyone whom the Lord our God calls
> to him."

Acts 2:39

Peter's sermon concludes with a convincing proclamation that all those who hear the promise can receive the promise. The old prophetic past and the recent resurrection are both made present and personal by the Holy Spirit.

Do you ever think that God's promises are for others, but somehow not for you?

PRAYER: Dear God, I want to hear every word you speak and every story you tell as a personal promise. I believe what you say and receive you gladly. Thank you for your gift of the Holy Spirit. *Amen.*

"Persons Were Added"

READ *Acts 2:40–42*

So those who welcomed his message were
baptized, and that day about three
thousand persons were added.

Acts 2:41

In a single day the small congregation of 120 grew
to a company of 3,000. The growth (like a mustard seed, like leaven) has continued, until today
every tongue and nation have people who listen
to the apostolic teaching, participate in our Lord's
life, and pray.

What Christians do you know in other lands?

PRAYER: "Blest river of salvation, Pursue thy on-
ward way; Flow thou to every nation, Nor in thy
richness stay: Stay not till all the lowly Triumphant reach their home; Stay not till all the holy
Proclaim, 'The Lord is come'" (Samuel F. Smith,
"The Morning Light Is Breaking"). *Amen.*

"As Any Had Need"

READ *Acts* 2:43—45

All who believed were together and had all
things in common; they would sell their
possessions and goods and distribute the
proceeds to all, as any had need.

Acts 2:44—45

Every true Christian community is a training center, in which we learn to discard our old habits of
getting all we can for ourselves, and acquire motives and means for giving all we can to others.

How has Christ changed your attitude toward
your possessions?

PRAYER: Dear God, you are Lord of my heart; be
also Lord of my bank account. Teach me your
merciful and gracious ways in all that I do, including the ways I spend my money and use my
possessions. *Amen.*

"Glad and Generous Hearts"

READ *Acts* 2:46–47

Day by day, as they spent much time
together in the temple, they broke bread
at home and ate their food with glad and
generous hearts. . . .

Acts 2:46

The results of the Church's first sermon are remarkable: surging gladness, reckless generosity, accelerating praise. When men and women receive God's spirit, they find themselves able to receive each other too, and are made into a community that lives to the glory of God.

In what ways is your church similar to this? In what ways dissimilar?

PRAYER: Powerfully and freely move through my church, O God, so that as we meet to hear your word, sing your praises, and present our offerings we may be known for our gladness and munificence—a church that faithfully believes your promises and generously lives in love. *Amen.*

"Walking and Leaping and Praising"
READ Acts 3:1–10

Jumping up, he stood and began to walk,
    and he entered the temple with them,
    walking and leaping and praising God.

Acts 3:8

The man healed at the Beautiful Gate is an "Every-man" of Christian response. "Hear him ye deaf; His praise, ye dumb, your loosened tongues employ; ye blind, behold your Savior come; and leap, ye lame, for joy!" (Charles Wesley, "O for a Thousand Tongues to Sing").

What is your favorite way of praising God?

PRAYER: What a wonderful way to express praise, O God! As I receive your great gifts of salvation, of wholeness, of love, may I be as expressive in gesture and act, so that those I meet may know the gladness that you create by your Spirit. In Jesus' name. *Amen.*

"The Faith That Is Through Jesus"
READ Acts 3:11–16

"And by faith in his name, his name itself
has made this man strong, whom you
see and know; and the faith that is
through Jesus has given him this perfect
health in the presence of all of you."

Acts 3:16

The crisp, concise witness to Jesus as the source of
new life prevents wandering speculation and distracting detours. Peter leads the crowd's aroused
curiosity away from the miracle to a point of attention on Jesus Christ.

If you were permitted only a single sentence to
explain what God has done for you, how would
you say it?

PRAYER: Father, when I have a chance to give witness to you, keep me to the point. Don't let me
wander through all the corridors of my own feelings and opinions. There is something very important to say; don't let me take too long to say it,
for Jesus' sake. *Amen.*

JULY 23

"Times of Refreshing"
READ *Acts* 3:17–26

". . . so that times of refreshing may come
from the presence of the Lord, and that
he may send the Messiah appointed for
you, that is, Jesus. . . ."

Acts 3:20

A religion that drives us to doomsday seriousness
and relentlessly insists on moral sweat, whatever
else it is, is not the gospel. The atmosphere here is
different: these are "times of refreshing." Jesus is
here "to bless you" (v. 26).

To you, what is most refreshing about the
gospel?

PRAYER: Lord God, you made a world of beauty to
tell your glory and fashioned a way of salvation to
share your love. Help me to add sounds of gladness to the happy praises of your people, through
Jesus Christ. *Amen.*

JULY 24

"Much Annoyed"

READ *Acts* 4:1–4

> While Peter and John were speaking to the
> people, the priests, the captain of the
> temple, and the Sadducees came to them,
> much annoyed because they were
> teaching the people and proclaiming
> that in Jesus there is the resurrection of
> the dead.
>
> *Acts* 4:1–2

Some leaders control and engineer people's spiritual lives to conform to their own ideas of decency and usefulness. Anyone who doesn't fit their job description of the "proper religious personality" is removed. God seems to delight in annoying them by upsetting their neat profile charts.

Are you ever annoyed at the way other people witness to Jesus?

PRAYER: Father, you know how narrow-minded I get sometimes, how I want everyone to think and speak and act just the way I do. Especially in church! Forgive me. I want to develop an appreciation for every variety of praise and witness that you create in others. *Amen.*

"No Other Name"

READ *Acts* 4:5–12

"There is salvation in no one else, for there is no other name under heaven given among mortals by which we must be saved."

Acts 4:12

Witness does not consist in explaining or defending one's own actions but in announcing God's actions. It is not a rehearsal of human possibilities or an exposition of human goodness but a single-minded testimony to Jesus.

Has anyone asked you recently for an explanation of your Christian behavior?

PRAYER: You are the one who is at work in this world, Almighty God, not me. I want my words and gestures to refer to you, not call attention to myself. It will hardly matter to people if they remember my name; it makes all the difference if they know yours. *Amen.*

JULY 26

"Companions of Jesus"

READ *Acts* 4:13

Now when they saw the boldness of Peter
and John and realized that they were
uneducated and ordinary men, they
were amazed and recognized them as
companions of Jesus.

Acts 4:13

Alert association with Jesus results in a life that is
more influenced by God than by human beings, a
daily existence in which God's presence, not humankind's, is the overpowering reality.

Do you ever hesitate in an act of Christian obedience for fear of disapproval or opposition?

PRAYER: God, when the counsel of mortals conflicts with the convictions born in me by your
Spirit, grant the grace of an unhesitating witness
to your word, in Jesus Christ. *Amen.*

"Cannot Keep from Speaking"
READ Acts 4:14–22

". . . for we cannot keep from speaking
about what we have seen and heard."

Acts 4:20

The cure for apathetic Christian witness is not a rehearsal of principles (why we should witness) nor a training in techniques (how to witness), but simply a participation in firsthand faith experience. Then witness bursts forth as a blossom from a bud.

What does it take to stop you from showing what you know of Christ?

PRAYER: Lord Jesus, in this moment of prayer, impress me with your love in such a way that I cannot hide its effects in my actions. Speak your word of salvation in such a way that it will be evident in this day's speech. *Amen.*

"Why Did the Gentiles Rage?"

READ *Acts* 4:23–31

"'Why did the Gentiles rage,
and the peoples imagine vain things?
The kings of the earth took their stand,
and the rulers have gathered together
against the Lord and against his Messiah.'"

Acts 4:25b–26

Herod and Pilate had done their best (or worst) and the word of God was stronger than ever. Nothing the world could throw against the gospel made a dent in it. Each confrontation was fresh evidence of the Spirit's invincibility. Every conflict made the apostolic witness bolder.

What psalm do Peter and John quote in their prayer?

PRAYER: "O where are kings and empires now Of old that went and came? But, Lord, Thy Church is praying yet, A thousand years the same. Unshaken as eternal hills, Immovable she stands, A mountain that shall fill the earth, A house not made by hands" (Arthur Cleveland Coxe, "O Where Are Kings and Empires Now"). *Amen.*

"One Heart and Soul"

READ *Acts* 4:32–37

Now the whole group of those who
    believed were of one heart and soul, and
    no one claimed private ownership of any
    possessions, but everything they owned
    was held in common.

Acts 4:32

Avarice-clenched fists, contracted for hitting and
holding, are relaxed into love-opened hands, supple for helping and sharing. In the Christian community we learn to relinquish our hold on what
we supposed were our possessions in order to
manage God's gifts for others.

In what ways did the early Christians show
their unity?

PRAYER: Father of creation, I have much yet to
learn about material goods. I keep thinking of
them as mine; you keep showing me that they are
yours. You are the owner and I am the manager:
help me to remember who owns what, and keep
me diligent in my stewardship. *Amen.*

"Kept Back Some of the Proceeds"

READ *Acts* 5:1–6

> But a man named Ananias, with the
> consent of his wife Sapphira, sold a
> piece of property; with his wife's
> knowledge, he kept back some of the
> proceeds, and brought only a part and
> laid it at the apostles' feet.
>
> *Acts* 5:1–2

Ananias and Sapphira were attracted to the warmth
and exhilaration of the Christian community and
wanted to participate in its blessings. Unwilling, though, to participate in its origins (the Holy
Spirit), they fabricated an imitation act of discipleship by copying from Barnabas. But it didn't work.

What did Ananias hope to gain from his deceit?

PRAYER: You, O God, show me the impossibility
of deceit and chicanery in the life of the Spirit.
Nothing can be copied, nothing can be faked. Do
your original work in me, making a life unique in
love and praise, in and through Jesus Christ. Amen.

"Put the Spirit of the Lord to the Test?"
READ Acts 5:7–11

> Then Peter said to her, "How is it that you
> have agreed together to put the Spirit of
> the Lord to the test? Look, the feet of
> those who have buried your husband are
> at the door, and they will carry you out."
>
> Acts 5:9

The enormity of the punishment cannot be accounted for on ethical grounds. Ananias and Sapphira's connivance did not hurt anyone. But the work of the Spirit was sabotaged. An attempt to manipulate and control God was substituted for a faith that is expectantly open to whatever the Creator Spirit might choose to do.

Have you ever attempted to deceive God? How?

PRAYER: God of mercy and might, expose conspiratorial tendencies within me that scheme to avoid the cross and sidestep discipleship. Why am I, even in church, always looking for a bargain, shopping around for cheap grace? Forgive me. *Amen.*

AUGUST 1

"Signs and Wonders"
READ *Acts 5:12–16*

Now many signs and wonders were done
among the people through the apostles.
And they were all together in Solomon's
Portico.

Acts 5:12

The life of the early Christian community shows
every sign of being continuous with the life of
Christ. The Founder is reproduced in his follow-
ers. Nothing that Jesus began stopped with him:
everything continued, even as he had promised,
in the lives of the believers.

Why were some too timid to join the Christian
community?

PRAYER: I thank you, Lord, that I have not only a
great heritage to look back upon in gratitude, but
a glorious present to celebrate and enjoy. Continue to do your work among your people, and
add believers to your Church. *Amen.*

"Opened the Prison Doors"
READ *Acts* 5:17–20

> But during the night an angel of the Lord
> opened the prison doors, brought them
> out, and said, "Go, stand in the temple
> and tell the people the whole message
> about this life."
>
> *Acts* 5:19–20

God has good news for us. The jealousy of rivals cannot silence it nor can prison walls suppress it. God always provides the means by which "the whole message about this life" will be spoken and heard.

Compare this with Psalm 107:10–16.

PRAYER: God, what seems like a dead end to me is, by your grace, a wide highway; what I experience as wretchedness is the very place in which you demonstrate deliverance. Increase my faith, so that I will meet setbacks with expectations, wondering how you will use them for your glory. *Amen.*

"Teaching the People"

READ *Acts 5:21–26*

Then someone arrived and announced,
   "Look, the men whom you put in
   prison are standing in the temple and
   teaching the people!"

Acts 5:25

The salvation accomplished in the death of Jesus and the new life flowing from his resurrection provide a new basis, so that every part of life can be lived in conscious, intelligent response to the truth that has entered our lives in Jesus Christ.

Why were the Jewish leaders so hostile?

PRAYER: Lord of all truth, I place my mind in your service: give me a most thorough knowledge of the ways of your salvation. I want to comprehend all the truth you have for me in Jesus. *Amen.*

"We Must Obey God"

READ *Acts* 5:27–32

> But Peter and the apostles answered, "We
> must obey God rather than any human
> authority."
>
> *Acts* 5:29

Most of us, most of the time, act in ways designed
to earn the support and admiration of our peers.
We like to be liked. But there is another, and better, way—to act in ways responsive to God.

Are there important people in your life whom
you are careful not to displease? Who are some of
them?

PRAYER: God, you know how solicitous I am of
the good opinion of others, and also how con-
stricted and cramped I become because of it. Help
me to find my chief motive in pleasing you, and
my chief happiness in enjoying your good pleasure. *Amen.*

AUGUST 5

"Gamaliel"

READ *Acts* 5:33–39

When they heard this, they were enraged
and wanted to kill them. But a Pharisee
in the council named Gamaliel, a teacher
of the law, respected by all the people,
stood up and ordered the men to be put
outside for a short time.

Acts 5:33–34

Gamaliel **did** not try to tell God how to work his
salvation, nor pretend to know all the ways in
which God might work his will in the world. The
combination of modesty and openness is as rare
as it is exemplary.

How can Gamaliel's example be put to use in
your life?

PRAYER: Why, O God, is it so hard for me to believe that you use people I don't like to bring
about your salvation? Why do I so confidently put
down everyone who appears to me to be wrong-
headed? *Amen.*

"Considered Worthy to Suffer"
READ Acts 5:40–42

As they left the council, they rejoiced that
they were considered worthy to suffer
dishonor for the sake of the name.

Acts 5:41

We ordinarily interpret suffering either as an acci-
dent we didn't deserve or as a punishment we did.
The apostles have a new insight: they see suffering
as the privilege of those entrusted with speaking
and demonstrating God's salvation in the world.
They find themselves participating in the suffer-
ings of Christ, and are glad.

What good do you see in suffering?

PRAYER: Transform my attitude toward suffering,
dear Christ, so that it becomes for me a means by
which I learn and share your salvation. Help me
to treat it not as something to be avoided at all
costs, but as part of the cost by which all things
are met redemptively in you. *Amen.*

"Seven Men of Good Standing"
READ Acts 6:1–6

"Therefore, friends, select from among
yourselves seven men of good standing,
full of the Spirit and of wisdom, whom
we may appoint to this task. . . ."

Acts 6:3

The Church is not permitted to choose between "preaching the word of God" and "waiting on tables." The first nurtures a relationship with God; the second develops love for neighbor. The early Christians found a way to provide leadership in each area so that neither was emphasized at the expense of the other.

How does your church provide for the two biblical emphases of ministry?

PRAYER: Father, I thank you for those who devote themselves to "prayer and to serving the word," and I thank you for others, "full of the Spirit and of wisdom," who "wait on tables." I need them both. Amen.

"The Word of God Continued to Spread"
READ *Acts* 6:7

> The word of God continued to spread; the
> number of the disciples increased greatly
> in Jerusalem, and a great many of the
> priests became obedient to the faith.
>
> *Acts* 6:7

The word of God, like the seed in Jesus' parable,
had been planted in good soil and now was growing to maturity. The "full grain" of conversion
and discipleship was becoming visible.

How do you measure growth in the church?

PRAYER: Bear good fruit in me, O God. Let your
words, which I have hidden in my heart, grow
and bear fruit. And not only in me but also in this
community: nurture the hidden process of germi-
nation and hasten the harvest, for the sake of Jesus
Christ. *Amen.*

AUGUST 9

"Stephen"

READ *Acts* 6:8–15

Stephen, full of grace and power, did great
wonders and signs among the people.

Acts 6:8

Stephen, one of the seven chosen to "wait on
tables," also gave verbal witness of high effectiveness. The Holy Spirit is able to use all forms of
witness—whether table ministry or pulpit ministry—to bring people's attention to Jesus Christ.

What are the key words used to describe
Stephen?

PRAYER: "Empower the hands and hearts and wills
Of friends both near and far, Who battle with the
body's ills And wage Thy holy war. O Father, look
from heaven and bless, Where'er Thy servants be,
Their works of pure unselfishness, Made conse-
crate to Thee" (Hardwicke D. Rawnsley, "Father,
Whose Will Is Life and Good," in *The Hymnbook*,
p. 309). *Amen.*

"Are These Things So?"

READ *Acts 7:1–8*

Then the high priest asked him, "Are these
  things so?"

Acts 7:1

Called before a Jewish council to defend his Christian acts and words, Stephen begins by talking of
Abraham. What the council members supposed
was a modern invention was in fact the oldest
truth in their creed. Those who interpreted faith
in Christ as opposing Jewish experience simply
weren't paying attention to Abraham.

What is the most significant thing about
Abraham?

PRAYER: God of our ancestors, you have led your
people across every kind of terrain and through
every kind of weather. You know your way
around the pains and difficulties of soul and society. Give me the long look, which sees victories of
faith and triumphs of love, that I may be steady
and sure in my walk with you. *Amen.*

"But God Was with Him"

READ *Acts* 7:9–16

"The patriarchs, jealous of Joseph, sold
him into Egypt; but God was with him,
and rescued him from all his afflictions,
and enabled him to win favor and to
show wisdom when he stood before
Pharaoh, king of Egypt, who appointed
him ruler over Egypt and over all his
household."

Acts 7:9–10

Joseph was cited in the early Christians' preaching
as evidence that God could use any kind of hostility and any sort of disaster for his redemptive purposes. Nothing that mortals do can thwart, finally,
what God will do in redemption.

Compare Stephen's summary of Joseph with
Genesis 45:7–8.

PRAYER: Lord, I know that your ways are sover-
eign and your will triumphant. Show me how
you will use the difficulties in my life to develop
your salvation. Complete your providence in me,
through Jesus Christ. *Amen.*

"Increased and Multiplied"

READ *Acts 7:17–22*

"But as the time drew near for the fulfillment
of the promise that God had made to
Abraham, our people in Egypt increased
and multiplied. . . ."

Acts 7:17

Israel's Egyptian experience was remembered for
two things: Israel was immersed in the most developed culture of the ancient world, and Israel was
in bondage. It was the best place in the world to
be; it was the worst condition to be in. Out of that
best and worst, God made a new people.

Why is Moses important in Christian memory?

PRAYER: I know, Father, that nothing is as good as
it looks from a distance; and nothing is as bad as
it feels when I am in the middle of it. Protect me
from envy of remote goods; keep me from despair in immediate trouble. Lead me into your salvation. *Amen.*

"A Resident Alien in the Land of Midian"
READ *Acts 7:23–29*

"When he heard this, Moses fled and
  became a resident alien in the land of
  Midian. There he became the father of
  two sons."

Acts 7:29

Even the great Moses was misunderstood. "Beautiful before God" (Acts 7:20), he was just one more person to be envied by his compatriots. But God used the result of Hebrew resentment (the Midian exile) to prepare Moses for the greatest act of leadership in biblical history.

How was the time in Midian used by God to strengthen Moses?

PRAYER: You know, God, how prone I am to moods of sulkiness when I am misunderstood and rejected. Help me to remember that it is not human beings I am serving, but you, and that you can use any situation to nurture your way in me. *Amen.*

"Come Now"

READ *Acts* 7:30–34

"'I have surely seen the mistreatment of my
people who are in Egypt and have heard
their groaning, and I have come down to
rescue them. Come now, I will send you
to Egypt.'"

Acts 7:34

In his youth, Moses had been so full of his own
prowess, enamored perhaps with his Egyptian wisdom, and so full of righteous indignation that he
was of no use to God at all. Then the forty-year
exile did its work and Moses became quiet enough
to hear God speak, and composed enough to be
aware of God's presence. Not until Moses was ready
to be led by God was he fit to be a leader for God.

What is God's message to Moses?

PRAYER: Provide me, O God, with a time of apart-
ness, an exile of some sort, so that I can get away
from my own schemes and forget my own
strength long enough to become thoroughly
conscious of your presence, the holy ground on
which even now I stand. *Amen.*

"In Their Hearts They Turned Back to Egypt"
READ *Acts 7:35–43*

> "Our ancestors were unwilling to obey him;
> instead, they pushed him aside, and in
> their hearts they turned back to Egypt. . . ."
>
> *Acts 7:39*

As Stephen tells the Egyptian story, he chooses to emphasize not the wonders of God's deliverance but the incredibility of the people's rejection. God did what he promised—his people didn't. Is it possible that those who are listening to the sermon are doing the same thing?

What prophet does Stephen quote?

PRAYER: You repeat, great God, your mighty acts of deliverance; and I repeat my acts of rejection. Will your mercy never end? Will my wandering never quit? Will your mercy outlast my rebellion? *Amen.*

"What Kind of House Will You Build?"

READ *Acts 7:44–50*

"Yet the Most High does not dwell in
   houses made with human hands; as the
   prophet says,
  'Heaven is my throne,
  and the earth is my footstool.
  What kind of house will you build for
    me, says the Lord,
  or what is the place of my rest?'"

Acts 7:48–49

Even the greatest of humankind's works (the Solomonic temple is an example) are nothing to be proud of since God does not live in them anyhow. If history is good for anything, it is to remember God's mercy and our mistakes.

What good does it do to build a church?

PRAYER: "Gracious Spirit, dwell with me; I myself would gracious be; And with words that help and heal Would Thy life in mine reveal; And with actions bold and meek Would for Christ my Savior speak" (Thomas Toke Lynch, "Gracious Spirit, Dwell with Me"). *Amen.*

"Just as Your Ancestors Used to Do"
READ Acts 7:51–53

"You stiff-necked people, uncircumcised in
   heart and ears, you are forever opposing
   the Holy Spirit, just as your ancestors
   used to do."

Acts 7:51

The conclusion to Stephen's sermon connects centuries of stubborn willfulness (the obtuse rejection
of Moses was an instance) with the crucifixion of
Jesus. Stephen's congregation wasn't used to hearing history that way—they had always treated it as
a gallery of achievements in which they found
cause for pride.

What does "stiff-necked" mean?

PRAYER: God, I don't want to repeat, unknowingly,
the sins of my fathers. I want to walk in the steps
of their pilgrimage, not of their rebellion. I want
to learn what I can from their obedience, not
wander blindly in the circles of their disobedience. Amen.

"They Became Enraged"
READ Acts 7:54–60

When they heard these things, they
became enraged and ground their teeth
at Stephen.

Acts 7:54

They should have known that getting rid of the
preacher was the most ineffective method possible for silencing the message. That has been tried
many times and has yet to work. Killing a Christian
is like hammering a nail: as visibility decreases,
effectiveness increases.

In what ways was Stephen's death similar to our
Lord's crucifixion?

PRAYER: I am needlessly fearful, Lord: I fear that
sinners' anger will put out your love, that mob
unbelief will trample your salvation. You cancel
my fears with your peace, and I know that "all
will be well and all manner of things will be
well," (Julian of Norwich) even in Jesus Christ.
Amen.

"A Severe Persecution"

READ Acts 8:1–3

But Saul was ravaging the church by
entering house after house; dragging off
both men and women, he committed
them to prison.

Acts 8:3

Saul, it seems, had found his vocation: he would
serve God by getting rid of those with whom he
didn't agree. His motives were unassailable, his
energies superb; his only mistake was in not first
checking to see what God thought of his plans.

Why did Saul think the Christians were wrong?

PRAYER: Lord, how often I do the same thing—
charge off into the world thinking I am doing
something for you, but in fact working contrary
to your will. Help me today to get my directions
straight before I start acting and speaking in your
name. *Amen.*

"Those Who Were Scattered"
READ *Acts* 8:4–8

Now those who were scattered went from
place to place, proclaiming the word.
Acts 8:4

The persecutors, trying to extirpate Christians
from Jerusalem, scattered them everywhere. Like
the wind that sails dandelion umbrella seeds across
fences onto neighboring lawns, persecution
spread the Christian presence into "all the world,"
where it took root and formed new churches. The
result (unplanned!) of Jerusalem persecution was
Samaritan joy.

Why is Samaria an important city for Christians?

PRAYER: "Fierce may be the conflict, Strong may
be the foe, But the King's own army None can
overthrow; Round His standard ranging, Victory
is secure; For His truth unchanging Makes the triumph sure. Joyfully enlisting By Thy grace divine,
We are on the Lord's side, Savior, we are Thine"
(Frances Ridley Havergal, "Who Is on the Lord's
Side?"). *Amen.*

"Simon"

READ *Acts 8:9–13*

Now a certain man named Simon had
    previously practiced magic in the city
    and amazed the people of Samaria,
    saying that he was someone great.

Acts 8:9

Magic is a way of manipulating God (or spiritual
powers) for trivial or base purposes. Faith is just
the opposite: it is that response to God that lets
him do what he wills in us.

Do you think magic is still confused with faith?

PRAYER: Father, I come to you not to get my way,
but to get yours; not to acquire a means of im-
pressing my friends with my power, but to let you
make an eternal impression on me with your salvation. *Amen.*

"Your Silver Perish with You"

READ *Acts* 8:14–24

But Peter said to him, "May your silver
perish with you, because you thought
you could obtain God's gift with money!"

Acts 8:20

Simon had supposed that the gospel was merely a superior form of what he already had: a way to get God to do what he wanted, and to amaze others with his power. But the gospel is not anything like that. It is the trust in God that lets God do what he wills in us, and the obedience to walk where he leads us.

Why is the judgment on Simon so severe?

PRAYER: "My Jesus, as Thou wilt! O may Thy will be mine! Into Thy hand of love I would my all resign. Through sorrow or through joy, Conduct me as Thine own; And help me still to say, 'My Lord, Thy will be done'" (Benjamin Schmolck, "My Jesus, as Thou Wilt"). *Amen.*

"Many Villages of the Samaritans"

READ Acts 8:25

> Now after Peter and John had testified
> and spoken the word of the Lord, they
> returned to Jerusalem, proclaiming the
> good news to many villages of the
> Samaritans.
>
> Acts 8:25

In his Gospel Luke told the stories of the Good
Samaritan and the Grateful Samaritan; in the Acts
he makes it clear that the first missionary outreach
was to the Samaritans. We cannot bypass our
neighbors, even when we don't like them, *especially*
when we don't like them.

Do you have "Samaritan" neighbors?

PRAYER: Lead me, God, into places of meeting and
opportunities for witness with neighbors who
hold the middle ground I bypass or avoid, particularly those with whom I have little in common
and among whom I have felt out of place. Use me
to break down walls of separation and to develop
enclaves of community. *Amen.*

"Do You Understand What You Are Reading?"

READ Acts 8:26–31

So Philip ran up to it and heard him reading
the prophet Isaiah. He asked, "Do you
understand what you are reading?"

Acts 8:30

All who read scripture spend some of their time
being puzzled. Our Lord graciously provides us
with gifted guides to explain and interpret the
rich meanings of the gospel that are in scripture.

Who has been of particular help in guiding
your reading and study of scripture?

PRAYER: Holy Spirit, I thank you for your scriptures, full of light and abundant in promise; and I
thank you for those who have opened them up to
me in new ways so that I can read with understanding, and respond with obedience. *Amen.*

"Look, Here Is Water!"

READ *Acts* 8:32–40

> As they were going along the road, they
> came to some water; and the eunuch
> said, "Look, here is water! What is to
> prevent me from being baptized?"
>
> *Acts* 8:36

The Ethiopian was not as interested in learning something new as he was in living a new life. No reading of scripture is properly concluded until we ask, "What is to prevent my putting this into action in my life, right now?" Scripture is not provided to improve our minds, but to change our lives.

What, in your reading of scripture today, can be acted upon?

PRAYER: I don't want to become merely knowledgeable in scripture, dear God. I want to absorb it into my muscles and bones, into my reflexes and habits, so that what is written on the pages of my Bible gets acted out in my daily round. *Amen.*

"Why Do You Persecute Me?"

READ Acts 9:1–9

> He fell to the ground and heard a voice
> saying to him, "Saul, Saul, why do you
> persecute me?"
>
> *Acts 9:4*

It is not only evil persons who need to be converted, but good ones—like Saul, who had every reason to think that he was doing God's will. No matter what we do, whether from good or evil intent, it is wrong until confronted and changed by a relation with Jesus Christ.

Why did Saul think he was doing God's will in persecuting Christians?

PRAYER: Turn me around, O God; turn me from running so hard toward what I think is right that I miss the signs pointing to your will for me. Do whatever is necessary to get me to stop, look, and listen to what you have to say to me, in Jesus. *Amen.*

"I Have Chosen"

READ *Acts* 9:10–19

> But the Lord said to him, "Go, for he is an
> instrument whom I have chosen to bring
> my name before Gentiles and kings and
> before the people of Israel. . . ."
>
> *Acts* 9:15

The quickness of Ananias to accept Saul as a
brother is as remarkable as Saul's willingness to
accept Jesus as Lord—and just as important, for
Saul was to be the human link in the divine chain
of command by which the Gentiles ("all the
world") were to hear the gospel proclaimed.

Whom do you have difficulty accepting as
God's instrument?

PRAYER: Help me, God, to be like Ananias: responsive to your will, even when I don't understand it; willing to change my idea of another,
even when it doesn't make sense to me; ready to
pray for and help the person I was convinced was
both your enemy and mine. *Amen.*

AUGUST 28

"Confounded the Jews"
READ *Acts* 9:20–22

Saul became increasingly more powerful
and confounded the Jews who lived in
Damascus by proving that Jesus was the
Messiah.

Acts 9:22

Why should a person quit doing what he thinks is
best and begin doing what God thinks is best? It
doesn't make sense, and yet it happens over and
over and over again. Nothing is more inexplicable,
but still indisputable, than a Christian conversion.

What do you think were some of Saul's arguments?

PRAYER: I know, Lord Jesus, that you do not want
my good intentions or my best efforts, but my
repentance and my faith. Not the best I can do,
but the best you can do in me. Live your love and
salvation through me, and upset the gloomy fore-
casts of what others think about me. *Amen.*

"Plotted to Kill Him"

READ Acts 9:23–30

After some time had passed, the Jews
plotted to kill him. . . .

Acts 9:23

While the Jews plotted Saul's murder, the Christians were afraid of him and the Hellenists sought to kill him. Conversion, for Saul, was a dangerous business! Becoming a Christian put him (as it puts us all) not in a consensus majority, but in a reconciling minority.

Do you think Saul was surprised by the hostility?

PRAYER: "Must I be carried to the skies On flowery beds of ease, While others fought to win the prize, And sailed through bloody seas?" (Isaac Watts, "Am I a Soldier of the Cross," in *The Hymnbook*, p. 353). Amen.

"Increased in Numbers"

READ *Acts* 9:31

> Meanwhile the church throughout Judea,
> Galilee, and Samaria had peace and was
> built up. Living in the fear of the Lord
> and in the comfort of the Holy Spirit, it
> increased in numbers.
>
> *Acts* 9:31

Opposition did not destroy the church, nor conflict make the Christians anxious. They experienced peace, they walked in reverence, and they knew comfort. In the midst of persecutors in a confounded world, we have this remarkable picture of a church serene and Christians confident.

What effect does opposition have on you?

PRAYER: God of grace, you know how very frightened I become when I see the power of evil in the world, how very nervous I get when I realize how little influence I have. As I take a good look at the way your people have thrived in battle and prospered in conflict, hearten me with peace and brace me with comfort. *Amen.*

"Tabitha"

READ *Acts 9:32–43*

> Now in Joppa there was a disciple whose
> name was Tabitha, which in Greek is
> Dorcas. She was devoted to good works
> and acts of charity.

Acts 9:36

Was Tabitha as lithe and graceful as her name? Now, though, the nimble fingers and compassionate hands were still. Peter's visit showed how Jesus' resurrection interrupts cause-and-effect sequences that we accept as inevitable and surprises everyone with a new conclusion.

What surprises has the resurrection given you?

PRAYER: Lord, I accept too many things as the last word when they are only the next-to-last word. The last word is yours; and it is a word of life, not of death. All praise to the living God! *Amen.*

"Cornelius"

READ Acts 10:1–2

In Caesarea there was a man named
Cornelius, a centurion of the Italian
Cohort, as it was called.

Acts 10:1

God will use Cornelius as a gate between Jew and
Gentile, between the concentrated center of Jewish Christianity and the worldwide orbit of Roman
civilization. Cornelius occupies the key position in
the story of evangelism.

What qualified Cornelius for his key role?

PRAYER: Father, what in me can you use to accomplish your will—what circumstances of birth, what
qualities of character? Do I have a place in your
plan? Show me what it is; keep me alert to your
signals and obedient to your commands. *Amen.*

"Send Men to Joppa"

READ *Acts* 10:3–8

"Now send men to Joppa for a certain
Simon who is called Peter; he is lodging
with Simon, a tanner, whose house is by
the seaside."

Acts 10:5–6

Even the greatest ventures of faith begin in the
simplest acts of obedience. The interchange between Peter and Cornelius would be used by the
Holy Spirit as a hinge to open the door of the
gospel to "all the world." Cornelius, oblivious to
the grand strategy, nevertheless made it possible
by his willingness to carry out the thoroughly
prosaic order, "Send men to Joppa."

Do you know how far it was from Caesarea to
Joppa?

PRAYER: God, when I excuse my disobedience
and inattention by saying that where I am and
who I am are so insignificant that it can't make
much difference anyway, ignore my excuses and
repeat your commands, through Jesus Christ.
Amen.

"On the Roof to Pray"
READ *Acts* 10:9–16

About noon the next day, as they were on
their journey and approaching the city,
Peter went up on the roof to pray.

Acts 10:9

Cornelius and Peter shared a habit of prayer. Even
though everything else about them was different—
their race, their religion, their work—because
they both prayed, God was able to put them together in common cause.

Do you have someone with whom you pray?

PRAYER: O God, when I pray, even though I am
alone, I know that I become a member of a great
company, unknown to me by sight and sound, ar-
rayed in your presence. Use my prayer to make
common cause with them in doing your work in
this world. *Amen.*

"Greatly Puzzled"

READ *Acts* 10:17–20

Now while Peter was greatly puzzled about
what to make of the vision that he had
seen, suddenly the men sent by Cornelius
appeared. They were asking for Simon's
house and were standing by the gate.

Acts 10:17

True prayer is never a pious disguise for otherwise
base pursuits. Nor is it ever a retreat from conflict
into a cave of serenity. Because prayer often leads
into new and unfamiliar territory, it hones the
growing edge of discipleship.

What don't you understand of God's will?

PRAYER: Dear God, build courage in me so that I
may not turn away timidly from what I do not yet
understand, nor shrink from engaging in acts
whose import I do not yet fathom. For Jesus' sake.
Amen.

"Directed"

READ *Acts* 10:21–23

They answered, "Cornelius, a centurion,
an upright and God-fearing man, who is
well spoken of by the whole Jewish
nation, was directed by a holy angel to
send for you to come to his house and
to hear what you have to say."

Acts 10:22

We are not locked into the cause-effect patterns of
either physical or psychological laws. But neither
are we left to the mercy of random chance. The
Holy Spirit is active in our lives to bring about en-
counters, to open up conversations, and to prepare events that evoke new obedience as we live
out God's purpose for us.

What new truth has God directed you into
lately?

PRAYER: "O Spirit of the Lord, prepare All the
round earth her God to meet; Breathe Thou abroad
like morning air, Till hearts of stone begin to
beat" (James Montgomery, "O Spirit of the Living
God"). *Amen.*

"I Am Only a Mortal"
READ Acts 10:23–26

On Peter's arrival Cornelius met him, and
falling at his feet, worshiped him. But
Peter made him get up, saying, "Stand
up; I am only a mortal."

Acts 10:25–26

Peter, at the center of the "new thing" that God
was doing, could easily have taken the role of the
pioneer and accepted the honors offered to a
brave genius in faith. Apparently it didn't even
occur to him. His rejection of a position of privilege was spontaneous.

Whom are you tempted to idolize?

PRAYER: God, idolatry and contempt alternate as
temptations. Give me the maturity to neither look
up to others nor look down upon them, but to
meet them eye-to-eye as companions in faith.
Amen.

"But God"

> . . . and he said to them, "You yourselves know that it is unlawful for a Jew to associate with or to visit a Gentile; but God has shown me **that** I should not call anyone profane or unclean."
>
> *Acts* 10:28

When Peter entered Cornelius's house, he violated a deeply ingrained respect for Jewish law and life-long habits of separation from Gentiles. But no list of arguments and no accumulation of culture were able to counter the bare, unadorned command of God. Peter was a man with a single authority.

What was God's command?

PRAYER: Majestic and Almighty Father, grant that neither the weight of old religious habits nor the authority of respected precedents will ever dilute my understanding of your command or divert me from responding to your promises, in Jesus Christ. *Amen.*

"In the Presence of God"

READ *Acts* 10:30–33

"Therefore I sent for you immediately, and you have been kind enough to come. So now all of us are here in the presence of God to listen to all that the Lord has commanded you to say."

Acts 10:33

The group in Cornelius's house was a model for all who gather for worship. The group had its genesis in prayer, was conscious of being assembled in the presence of God, and was attentive to what God would speak through his preaching servant. In such groups, still, God reveals his plans for loving the world and deploys his people for the work that will make it happen.

Are you acquainted with people similar to those in Cornelius's house?

PRAYER: When next I gather with brothers and sisters in Christ, O God, I want my attention centered on your word, my spirit aware of your presence, and my body ready for action in carrying out the commands that I hear in your gospel. Amen.

"No Partiality"

Then Peter began to speak to them: "I truly
understand that God shows no partiality,
but in every nation anyone who fears
him and does what is right is acceptable
to him."

Acts 10:34–35

Until we perceive, along with Peter, the essential
equality of all people, we are not ready for evangelism. We cannot tell another of Christ's salvation
from a standpoint of privilege or with a conscious-
ness of superiority.

What people do you have difficulty accepting
as equals?

PRAYER: God of the nations, Lord of the lost, dissolve the traditions that separate me from others
and so prevent me from speaking the personal,
convincing word of your acceptance and your
love. Help me to see each person I meet today in
the light of your affirming creation and your redeeming love. *Amen.*

"How God Anointed Jesus"
READ Acts 10:36–38

"That message spread throughout Judea,
 beginning in Galilee after the baptism
 that John announced: how God anointed
 Jesus of Nazareth with the Holy Spirit
 and with power; how he went about
 doing good and healing all who were
 oppressed by the devil, for God was
 with him."

Acts 10:37–38

The convincing demonstration of God's saving love for all humanity takes place in one man: Jesus of Nazareth. The universality of what God does is not announced in generalities, but in a single, powerful, particular person in whom we can examine each line of love and each motion of salvation.

How does Jesus convince you of God's love?

PRAYER: Thank you, Father, for Jesus. Thank you for his story in which I learn over and over again of the way your love works in me, and for his presence by which I share a life of salvation. Amen.

"Witnesses"

READ *Acts* 10:39–41

"We are witnesses to all that he did both in Judea and in Jerusalem. They put him to death by hanging him on a tree. . . ."

Acts 10:39

Witnesses don't make up the story of the gospel, nor are they responsible for its success. Nevertheless, they are in an awesome and critical position, for they link what God did in Jesus with what he will do in all who respond in faith.

How do you function as a witness?

PRAYER: "I love to tell the story Of unseen things above, Of Jesus and His glory, Of Jesus and His love. I love to tell the story, Because I know 'tis true; It satisfies my longings As nothing else could do" (Katherine Hankey, "I Love to Tell the Story"). *Amen.*

"Forgiveness of Sins"
READ *Acts* 10:42–43

"All the prophets testify about him that
everyone who believes in him receives
forgiveness of sins through his name."

Acts 10:43

The gospel is no muckraking exposé, but an invit-
ing hospitality. Evangelism is promise, not condemnation. Peter's sermon concludes at the point
where God's action in Jesus converges with humankind's need for forgiveness.

How is your life changed by forgiveness?

PRAYER: God, your great and gracious ways are
bright with hope and promises; I find your
centuries-long history of salvation directed
through me; I accept all you offer, through Jesus
Christ. *Amen.*

"Even on the Gentiles"

READ *Acts* 10:44–46

The circumcised believers who had come
with Peter were astounded that the gift
of the Holy Spirit had been poured out
even on the Gentiles. . . .

Acts 10:45

Our perceptions always lag behind God's revelations. Just when we think we have everything fig-
ured out, God does something new. Every fresh
outpouring of his Spirit pushes out the frontiers a
little farther.

What work of the Spirit has taken you by
surprise?

PRAYER: Father in heaven, when you work in others I am very frequently taken unawares, insensitive as I am to their readiness to respond to your
love. When that happens, change my surprise into
praise so that I am no longer an amazed spectator
but a grateful participant. *Amen.*

SEPTEMBER 14

"Baptized"

READ *Acts* 10:47–48

So he ordered them to be baptized in the
  name of Jesus Christ. Then they invited
  him to stay for several days.

Acts 10:48

The act of the Holy Spirit was acknowledged in
the rite of baptism. All acts of worship are, in one
way or another, variations on the awed confession, "Surely the LORD is in this place—and I did
not know it!" (Genesis 28:16). Worship doesn't
make God do something; it responds to what he
has been doing and is doing.

What did baptism mean to the early Christians?

PRAYER: "God bless the men and women Who
serve Him oversea; God raise up more to help
them To set the nations free, Till all the distant
people In every foreign place Shall understand
His Kingdom And come into His grace" (Percy
Dearmer, "Remember All the People," in *The Hymnbook*, p. 495). Amen.

SEPTEMBER 15

"Criticized"

READ Acts 11:1–3

So when Peter went up to Jerusalem, the
circumcised believers criticized him. . . .

Acts 11:2

Here is a model for healthy criticism: it originates
in genuine bewilderment, it is directed to the person involved, and it waits for an answer. Out of
such criticism, growth takes place and community deepens.

What recent act of criticism has been construc-
tive for you?

PRAYER: God, instead of rejecting or condemning
what I don't understand, I want to ask the right
questions in the right tone of voice so that my
puzzlement may develop into understanding.
Show me how to do this, through Jesus Christ my
Lord. *Amen.*

"Began to Explain"

READ Acts 11:4–10

Then Peter began to explain it to them,
 step by step, saying, "I was in the city of
 Joppa praying, and in a trance I saw a
 vision. There was something like a large
 sheet coming down from heaven, being
 lowered by its four corners; and it came
 close to me."

Acts 11:4–5

Peter's response to criticism from the Judean
brethren combined directness, candor, and orderliness. He neither resented nor dismissed the critics.
Explanation is an aspect of witness.

What experience is important for you to share
with another?

PRAYER: God, I often brush off the questions of
critics. Help me to provide clear explanations instead, explanations that show the ways you are
working out your plan of salvation among all
peoples, in all the world, through Jesus Christ.
Amen.

"Just as It Had upon Us"

READ *Acts* 11:11–15

"And as I began to speak, the Holy Spirit
fell upon them just as it had upon us at
the beginning."

Acts 11:15

If the work of the Holy Spirit surprises us by its
scope, it is still recognizable in its character. Whatever the form and whoever the recipient, it is always the same Spirit as was revealed in Jesus—in
his words and acts, his death and resurrection.

How can you identify the work of the Holy
Spirit?

PRAYER: Holy Spirit, expand my comprehension
and deepen my insight as you do your work of re-
generation in the world; and I will declare the
wideness of your mercy, the broadness of your
love. *Amen.*

"Even to the Gentiles"

READ *Acts 11:16–18*

When they heard this, they were silenced.
And they praised God, saying, "Then
God has given even to the Gentiles the
repentance that leads to life."

Acts 11:18

Peter's concise and unadorned witness was convincing. As the Jerusalem congregation listened, understanding developed into acceptance. When they spoke again, it was no longer in criticism but in praise.

What convinced them of Peter's authority?

PRAYER: "Eternal God, whose power upholds Both flower and flaming star, To whom there is no here nor there, No time, no near nor far, No alien race, no foreign shore, No child unsought, unknown: O send us forth, Thy prophets true, To make all lands Thine own!" (Henry Hallam Tweedy, "Eternal God, Whose Power Upholds"). *Amen.*

"A Good Man"

... for he was a good man, full of the Holy
Spirit and of faith. And a great many
people were brought to the Lord.

Acts 11:24

As the gentile communities of Christians came
into being, the Jerusalem church felt a responsi-
bility for guiding and nurturing their new life in
Christ. Barnabas, a trusted leader, was dispatched
for the pastoral work.

What were Barnabas's qualifications for pastoral work?

PRAYER: God, I thank you not only for brave and
courageous witnesses by whom I hear your word,
but also for good and faithful pastors by whom I
am established in your grace. I need them both,
and I give you thanks for both. In Jesus' name.
Amen.

"First Called 'Christians'"

READ *Acts* 11:25–26

> . . . and when he had found him, he
> brought him to **Antioch**. So it was that
> for an entire year they met with the
> church and taught a great many people,
> and it was in Antioch that the disciples
> were first called "Christians."

Acts 11:26

Naming is a way of making: we become what we are called. More than a label that identifies, the name is a power that shapes. "Christian" is the best of identities, and the most powerful of influences. All who live under its potency are "being changed into his likeness" (2 Cor. 3:18).

How would you define the word "Christian"?

PRAYER: Lord, you have called me what I am not yet, but what by your grace I am becoming I would honor the name by which I am honored; dear Christ, hallowed be your name. *Amen.*

"Relief to the Believers"
READ *Acts* 11:27–30

The disciples determined that according to
    their ability, each would send relief to
    the believers living in Judea. . . .

Acts 11:29

Offerings for relief are as biblical as invitations to
receive salvation. Bread for the hungry is a gospel
concern quite as much as the preaching of the
Word. Whenever Christians worship, they are responsible for both announcing the Truth and
demonstrating the Mercy.

What "relief to the believers" is your church
engaged in?

PRAYER: God, in Jesus you showed that you never
separate your loving concern for souls in need
from your loving compassion for bodies in distress. Neither do I want to separate my love, in my
money and my morals, in my witness and my
giving, I want to express all your love, through
Jesus Christ. *Amen.*

"Violent Hands"

READ *Acts* 12:1–5

About that time King Herod laid violent
  hands upon some who belonged to the
  church.

Acts 12:1

On the anniversary of Jesus' arrest and crucifix-
ion, James was executed and Peter imprisoned.
"Christians regarded themselves as sinners, and
other people regarded them as criminals"
(Charles Williams, *The Descent of the Dove* [New
York: Meridian Books, 1956], p. 20).

   Why was there opposition to the Christians?

PRAYER: "Lo! the hosts of evil round us Scorn Thy
Christ, assail His ways! From the fears that long
have bound us Free our hearts to faith and praise.
Grant us wisdom, grant us courage, For the living
of these days, For the living of these days" (Harry
Emerson Fosdick, "God of Grace and God of
Glory"). *Amen.*

"Suddenly an Angel"

READ *Acts* 12:6–9

Suddenly an angel of the Lord appeared
and a light shone in the cell. He tapped
Peter on the side and woke him, saying,
"Get up quickly." And the chains fell off
his wrists.

Acts 12:7

Peter, expecting death from his king, received life from his Lord. The angelic rescue was an application of the resurrection in the dungeon of imprisonment. It was no less real for seeming like a dream.

Why did Peter think he was seeing a vision?

PRAYER: Lord of resurrection, my expectations are formed by the worst that human beings can do, but my faith is formed by the best that you can do. Enable me to overcome the world, even as you did, in Jesus Christ. *Amen.*

"Rescued"

READ Acts 12:10–11

Then Peter came to himself and said, "Now
I am sure that the Lord has sent his angel
and rescued me from the hands of
Herod and from all that the Jewish
people were expecting."

Acts 12:11

People accustomed to getting verification of reality from newspaper reports and laboratory tests have no vocabulary for describing an act of salvation. Angel visitations are, from all accounts, quiet and unobserved. But the results are dramatic and historic.

Why was Peter, do you think, sure it was an angel?

PRAYER: Visit me, Holy Spirit, and free me from all that confines and restricts. Bring me into a broad place where I can stand with the great congregation and praise your saving acts, in the name of Father, Son, and Holy Spirit. *Amen.*

"Rhoda"

READ *Acts* 12:12–15

When he knocked at the outer gate, a maid
  named Rhoda came to answer.

Acts 12:13

The lovely spontaneity of Rhoda was instinctive in its priorities. She delayed her maid's work of unlatching the gate until she had completed her evangelical task of reporting the answered prayer. Joy is always a proper interruption of duty.

Was the praying in verse 12 a continuation of that in verse 5?

PRAYER: How much, O God, of what I recognize as your work in my life is fashioned out of the prayers of my friends? Thank you for their courage and persistence, for the strong prayers offered in the name of Jesus. *Amen.*

"Tell This to James"
READ *Acts* 12:16–17

He motioned to them with his hand to be
silent, and described for them how the
Lord had brought him out of the prison.
And he added, "Tell this to James and to
the believers." Then he left and went to
another place.

Acts 12:17

The work of the Spirit consisted in a subterranean
network that, in various homes and synagogues,
surfaced in pools of prayer and fountains of praise.
As Christians reported these to one another, a
kind of coherence became evident, a coherence
described in the word "church."

Who was James?

PRAYER: "Give the winds a mighty voice, Jesus
saves! Jesus saves! Let the nations now rejoice—
Jesus saves! Jesus saves! Shout salvation full and
free To each strand that ocean laves, This our song
of victory—Jesus saves! Jesus saves!" (Priscilla J.
Owens, "We Have Heard the Joyful Sound").
Amen.

"No Small Commotion"
READ *Acts* 12:18–19

> When morning came, there was no small
> commotion among the soldiers over
> what had become of Peter.
>
> *Acts* 12:18

Nothing is less effective than violence in solving a problem, yet it seems to have been the only method that Herod ever used. He killed his (supposed) enemy, James; now he kills his (supposed) friends, the soldiers. Each time without effect.

Compare and contrast this passage with Acts 12:1–2.

PRAYER: While "the nations conspire, and the peoples plot in vain" (Psalm 2:1), I put my trust in you, Almighty God. I will not fear, "though the earth should change, though the mountains shake in the heart of the sea; though its waters roar and foam, though the mountains tremble with its tumult" (Psalm 46:2–3). *Amen.*

"Not Given the Glory to God"

READ *Acts* 12:20–23

And immediately, because he had not given
the glory to God, an angel of the Lord
struck him down, and he was eaten by
worms and died.

Acts 12:23

At one moment Herod is acclaimed as "the voice
of a god"; in the next he is described as "eaten by
worms." What the crowd thought of him and
what he really was were very different. As usual,
the crowd was wrong.

What else do you know about Herod?

PRAYER: "Riches I heed not, nor man's empty
praise, Thou mine inheritance, now and always:
Thou and Thou only, first in my heart, High King
of heaven, my Treasure Thou art" (Mary Byrne,
trans., "Be Thou My Vision" (ancient Irish hymn)
in *The Hymnbook*, p. 303). *Amen.*

SEPTEMBER 29

"Advance and Gain"

READ *Acts* 12:24

But the word of God continued to advance
and gain adherents.

Acts 12:24

Luke contrasts the death of Herod with the life of
the church: the persecuting potentate, resplendent
in robes of royalty, was a worm-eaten corpse; the
persecuted church, furtive and harassed, flour-
ished as the gospel took form and bore fruits of
righteousness.

Summarize the action of chapter 12.

PRAYER: Eternal God, even as the arrogant are
brought to their knees by your mercy and the proud
are led to obeisance by your love, so bring me to the
point of adoration where all the stratagems of your
salvation converge in my heart, and are offered up
in praise, to the glory of Father, Son, and Holy
Spirit. *Amen.*

SEPTEMBER 30

"Completing Their Mission"
READ *Acts* 12:25

Then after completing their mission
  Barnabas and Saul returned to Jerusalem
  and brought with them John, whose
  other name was Mark.

Acts 12:25

While the foreground action has been centering on Peter, background actions have been going on that will lead into the next part of the story: Barnabas, Saul, and Mark were quietly and obediently being readied to take their places in leadership.

Are you impatient with preparation times?

PRAYER: God of grace, whenever I read these scriptures closely I realize that most of the action takes place behind the scenes—in years of praying preparations, in long stretches of hidden faithfulness. Help me to embrace in praise the obscure parts of my life as well as the clear signs of your favor. Amen.

"Set Apart"

READ Acts 13:1–3

While they were worshiping the Lord and
fasting, the Holy Spirit said, "Set apart
for me Barnabas and Saul for the work to
which I have called them."

Acts 13:2

The missionary movement, which can be said to
have begun at this moment, was launched not by
people in committee trying to figure out what
was best for the world, but by people in prayer
who were willing to do nothing ("fasting") until
God formed his intentions and will in them.

In what special ways are Paul and Barnabas
qualified for this work?

PRAYER: "God of the prophets! Bless the prophets'
sons; Elijah's mantle o'er Elisha cast; Each age its
solemn task may claim but once; Make each one
nobler, stronger than the last" (Denis Wortman,
"God of the Prophets"). *Amen.*

"Bar-Jesus"

READ Acts 13:4–12

When they had gone through the whole
island as far as Paphos, they met a
certain magician, a Jewish false prophet,
named Bar-Jesus.

Acts 13:6

Magic, as a form of religion, "makes crooked the
straight paths of the Lord" (Acts 13:10) by com-
plicating with abracadabra the powerful simplicities of the cross, and obscuring with mystification
the clear revelation of Jesus Christ.

How was Bar-Jesus a threat to the Christian
witness?

PRAYER: Grant me, God, clear-eyed discernment
so that I may not be dazzled by hucksters of spiritual remedies who promise a religion without a
cross. Keep my attention on the plain and lovely
simplicities of Christ crucified for my sins and
risen for my salvation. *Amen.*

OCTOBER 3

"Into the Synagogue"
READ *Acts* 13:13–15

... but they went on from Perga and came
to Antioch in Pisidia. And on the sabbath
day they went into the synagogue and
sat down.

Acts 13:14

The Jews, scattered by earlier persecutions, had
obediently maintained their sabbath worship
wherever they went so that there were synagogues
in most cities in the Greco-Roman world. As
places where God was taken seriously and scripture studied carefully, they were ideal sites for the
apostolic preaching.

Can you see the background of the synagogue
in your church?

PRAYER: I listen again, O God, for you to speak
your word to me out of scripture. Let my listening
become understanding, and my understanding
become faith, and my faith become discipleship,
through Jesus Christ. *Amen.*

OCTOBER 4

"Who Fear God, Listen"
READ *Acts* 13:16–25

So Paul stood up and with a gesture began
to speak: "You Israelites, and others who
fear God, listen."

Acts 13:16

Paul begins his sermon by rehearsing the events
that led up to the presentation of "a Savior, Jesus"
(v. 23). A people familiar with the way God has
worked in Israel will recognize the authenticity of
God's best and final work, Jesus.

How much of the history that Paul presents is
familiar to you?

PRAYER: I would be attentive to all that you have
done in past ages, great God. I would ponder
modes of salvation and meditate on people of
faith. Use the compost of this history to put nutri-
ents into my daily faith. *Amen.*

"Fulfilled for Us"

READ *Acts* 13:26–41

"And we bring you the good news that
what God promised to our ancestors he
has fulfilled for us, their children, by
raising Jesus; as also it is written in the
second psalm,
'You are my Son; today I have begotten
you.'"

Acts 13:32–33

All Paul's preaching has the phrase "fulfilled for
us" at its core. All that had been promised in
scripture and all that had been anticipated in the
great saving events of the past is now present,
actual, and accessible in Jesus, whom God had
raised from the dead.

What is fulfilled in Christ?

PRAYER: Father, I want to get the full impact of
your promise. I want to respond in faith with all
that you have prepared me for and experience in
love all that you have prepared for me, even now
in Jesus Christ. *Amen.*

"Urged Them"

READ *Acts 13:42–43*

When the meeting of the synagogue broke
up, many Jews and devout converts to
Judaism followed Paul and Barnabas,
who spoke to them and urged them to
continue in the grace of God.

Acts 13:43

No good sermon is ever complete in itself. It stimulates appetites that require repeated returns to the table of the Lord, and it uncovers needs that throw us into an increasingly conscious dependence upon the grace of Christ.

What results did last Sunday's sermon have in you?

PRAYER: "As pants the hart for cooling streams When heated in the chase, So longs my soul, O God, for Thee, and Thy refreshing grace. For Thee, my God, the living God, My thirsty soul doth pine; O when shall I behold Thy face, Thou Majesty divine!" ("As Pants the Hart for Cooling Streams," adapted from Psalm 42). *Amen.*

"Jealousy"

The next sabbath almost the whole city
    gathered to hear the word of the Lord.
But when the Jews saw the crowds,
    they were filled with jealousy; and
    blaspheming, they contradicted what
    was spoken by Paul.

Acts 13:44–45

Base and unworthy attitudes can originate in places of worship as easily and frequently as in any other place. A person who goes to church can leave it worse than when he or she entered.

Did you leave worship on Sunday better, or worse, than when you arrived?

PRAYER: When I next go to worship, dear God, make it for me a new beginning in adoration and a fresh renewal of love. Purge the roots of bitterness from my heart and banish jealous pride, for Jesus' sake. *Amen.*

"The Word of the Lord Spread"
READ *Acts* 13:48–52

Thus the word of the Lord spread
throughout the region.

Acts 13:49

Persecution was a spur in the flank of evangelism. Hostility in one town created the pressure that erupted as gladness and praise for the word of God in the next (v. 48). In such fashion the Holy Spirit turned "human wrath" to the praise of God (Psalm 76:10).

Compare this with Jesus' instructions in Mark 6:11.

PRAYER: You, Lord, who were despised and rejected by mortals and yet became Lord and Savior to the very people who denied and blasphemed your name, use my experiences of rejection in similar ways so that I may be a good witness to your glorious love. *Amen.*

"Divided"

READ Acts 14:1–7

> But the residents of the city were divided;
> some sided with the Jews, and some
> with the apostles.

Acts 14:4

The gospel illuminates a crossroads: Will we walk in the ways of pride, anxiously lugging all the baggage of self-importance? Or will we walk in the way of the cross, casting our burdens on the Lord, receiving forgiveness, and living in obedience by grace? "Once to every man and nation Comes the moment to decide" (James Russell Lowell, "Once to Every Man and Nation," in *The Hymnbook*, p. 361).

Why did some people oppose the apostles?

PRAYER: God, I make my choice to follow you; now guard me from distracting byways, keep me from faithlessly looking back, refresh me with courage when trials are severe, and fix my eyes on the goal, "looking to Jesus," in whose name I pray. *Amen.*

OCTOBER 10

"We Are Mortals"

READ *Acts* 14:8–18

> "Friends, why are you doing this? We are
> mortals just like you, and we bring you
> good news, that you should turn from
> these worthless things to the living God,
> who made the heaven and the earth and
> the sea and all that is in them."
>
> *Acts* 14:15

It is always easier to put people on a pedestal and
worship them as gods than to worship the God
who took the form of a servant, "poured out himself to death, and was numbered with the trans-
gressors" (Isaiah 53:12).

Do you ever "worship" human beings in place
of God?

PRAYER: "The dearest idol I have known, Whate'er
that idol be, Help me to tear it from Thy throne,
And worship only Thee. So shall my walk be close
with God, Calm and serene my frame; So purer
light shall mark the road That leads me to the
Lamb" (William Cowper, "O for a Closer Walk
with God"). *Amen.*

"Through Many Persecutions"
READ *Acts* 14:19–23

> There they strengthened the souls of the
> disciples and encouraged them to
> continue in the faith, saying, "It is
> through many persecutions that we must
> enter the kingdom of God."
>
> *Acts* 14:22

A gospel that boldly sets the cross of Christ at the center of its message also courageously accepts the cross of discipleship as part of its daily routines. Difficulties and suffering are not problems for which the gospel provides an escape, but part of a reality that the Christian experiences in triumph.

What tribulations are the common lot of Christians?

PRAYER: Lord, I sometimes think that my troubles are a punishment because I haven't done a very good job of being your child; at other times I think they occur because you haven't done a very good job of being my Lord. Show me the folly of such thoughts and convince me of the wisdom of the cross, on which you accomplished my salvation and beneath which I take my stand. *Amen.*

"The Work That They Had Completed"
READ *Acts* 14:24–28

From there they sailed back to Antioch,
    where they had been commended to the
    grace of God for the work that they had
    completed.

Acts 14:26

The first missionary journey was now completed.
Paul and Barnabas had traveled about a thousand
miles preaching, teaching, and healing. The
Antioch church, which earlier had commissioned
them for the work, now heard the reports that
God had, in fact, "opened a door of faith for the
Gentiles" (v. 27).

Review the beginning of this journey in Acts
13:1–3.

PRAYER: Grant, God, that I may, this day, work
obediently, love consistently, continue faithfully,
and praise joyfully. And when this day's tasks are
completed, prepare me for tomorrow's. *Amen.*

"The Custom of Moses"

READ *Acts* 15:1–5

> Then certain individuals came down from
> Judea and were teaching the brothers,
> "Unless you are circumcised according
> to the custom of Moses, you cannot be
> saved."

Acts 15:1

Does a person have to be religious before becoming a Christian? Are there prerequisites (undergraduate courses!) to be fulfilled before we can enroll in the finished work of salvation by the grace of Jesus Christ? Must one become a Jew before becoming a Christian? These are the questions that the Jerusalem church prepares to debate.

In what way are these questions contemporary?

PRAYER: Lord God, forgive me when I let the customs and conventions of my church get in the way of what you have to say to those you are calling to repentance and faith. *Amen.*

"Why Are You Putting God to the Test?"

READ *Acts 15:6–11*

"Now therefore why are you putting God to
the test by placing on the neck of the
disciples a yoke that neither our ancestors
nor we have been able to bear?"

Acts 15:10

God, not humankind, runs the business of salvation. God, not his churches, determines how men
and women shall receive his eternal life. When we
interpose our protocols of salvation we only intro-
duce confusion and add burdens.

What evidence does Peter use to support his
argument?

PRAYER: Father, instead of insisting that others
duplicate the steps of preparation through which
you have led me, I want to simply accept others
where they are, share the life you have given me
by grace, and trust you to be their Lord and Savior
in whatever way you will, in Jesus Christ. *Amen.*

"James"

After they finished speaking, James replied,
  "My brothers, listen to me. Simeon has
  related how God first looked favorably
  on the Gentiles, to take from among
  them a people for his name."

Acts 15:13–14

James, pastor to the Jerusalem congregation, immediately recognized the truth of Paul and Barnabas's witness. He was convinced not by their arguments or rhetorical skills, but because the word of God in scripture validated what they said.

From which scriptures does James quote?

PRAYER: Give me, Lord, by means of your scriptures, such a grounding in your ways and familiarity with your will that I will be able to see additional things you are doing and hear the latest words you are speaking among those with whom I find myself. *Amen.*

"No Further Burden"
READ *Acts* 15:22–29

"For it has seemed good to the Holy Spirit
and to us to impose on you no further
burden than these essentials: that you
abstain from what has been sacrificed to
idols and from blood and from what is
strangled and from fornication. If you
keep yourselves from these, you will do
well. Farewell."

Acts 15:28–29

Against those who would center life in human
religious observances, the Christians centered it
in what God did in Christ. If certain prohibitions
are, for the time being, expedient, they must be
few and peripheral. For life's arena is grace and its
action is Christ.

Compare this passage with Paul's counsel in
1 Corinthians 8:7–13.

PRAYER: Almighty God, you have given me vast
freedom and leisured liberty in which to receive
and share your love. In my enjoyment of grace,
grant that I may be neither insensitive to the need
for guidelines nor uncharitable with those who
announce them. *Amen.*

"Rejoiced at the Exhortation"
READ *Acts* 15:30–35

So they were sent off and went down to
Antioch. When they gathered the
congregation together, they delivered
the letter. When its members read it,
they rejoiced at the exhortation.

Acts 15:30–31

Would the Antioch Christians be divided from
their brothers and sisters in Jerusalem? Care was
taken to prevent that when the visit of Paul and
Barnabas was reciprocated by the visit of Judas
and Silas. The visits developed appreciation and
understanding, forging joyous bonds of kinship
between the two communities of believers.

Why did the Antioch Christians rejoice?

PRAYER: Lord, I want to convey the messages and
report the news that help bind people together in
communities of praise and adoration. *Amen.*

"They Parted Company"

READ *Acts 15:36–41*

The disagreement became so sharp that
they parted company; Barnabas took
Mark with him and sailed away to
Cyprus. But Paul chose Silas and set out,
the believers commending him to the
grace of the Lord.

Acts 15:39–40

If it is, at first, disappointing to find that the great
preachers of reconciliation were not able to keep
peace among themselves, it is, on reflection, an
encouragement. The apostolic leaders were not exempt from the temptations that face us each day,
nor incapable of the failures that mire us in guilt.

Whose side would you have taken in the disagreement?

PRAYER: God, I'm not glad that Paul and Barnabas
had that fight, but I'm glad to know about it—to
know that their mission was not conditional on
their virtue but on your grace, and to know that
you used them not because they were sinless but
because they received your forgiveness for their
sin. *Amen.*

"Timothy"

READ *Acts 16:1–5*

> Paul went on also to Derbe and to Lystra,
> where there was a disciple named
> Timothy, the son of a Jewish woman
> who was a believer; but his father was a
> Greek.

Acts 16:1

Timothy, an early convert of Paul's ministry, became a trusted co-worker and, at the end, the person Paul most wanted to have with him during the final imprisonment: "Do your best to come before winter" (2 Timothy 4:21).

Read Paul's description of Timothy in 1 Corinthians 4:17.

PRAYER: Dear Lord, receive my thanks for companions in discipleship, friends who share a loyalty to your will, who lighten the difficulties of tribulation and deepen the moments of joy. In Jesus' name. *Amen.*

"Come Over to Macedonia"
READ Acts 16:6–10

> During the night Paul had a vision: there
> stood a man of Macedonia pleading with
> him and saying, "Come over to
> Macedonia and help us."
>
> *Acts 16:9*

The vision of the Macedonian calling for help has
become a signature of the missionary movement:
in every land the deepest human cry is for a personal meeting with the God who is personal to us
in Jesus Christ.

Where is Macedonia?

PRAYER: "Arm of the Lord, awake, awake! Put on
Thy strength, the nations shake, And let the
world, adoring, see Triumphs of mercy wrought
by Thee. Almighty God, Thy grace proclaim In
every clime of every name; Let adverse powers before Thee fall, And crown the Savior Lord of all"
(William Shrubsole, "Arm of the Lord, Awake!").
Amen.

"Lydia"

READ *Acts* 16:11–15

> A certain woman named Lydia, a worshiper
> of God, was listening to us; she was from
> the city of Thyatira and a dealer in purple
> cloth. The Lord opened her heart to listen
> eagerly to what was said by Paul.

Acts 16:14

The gospel expands across the Aegean Sea to the shores of Europe, where the merchant Lydia is the first convert. Two things are wonderful in her: her open heart with which she received God's word and her open house in which she received her new friends in Christ.

Why is this trip important?

PRAYER: Grant, Lord, that the generosity I admire in others may become functional in me: an open-hearted readiness to receive your word, an open-handed friendship in receiving your children in my home. *Amen.*

"But Paul, Very Much Annoyed"
READ Acts 16:16–18

She kept doing this for many days. But
   Paul, very much annoyed, turned and
   said to the spirit, "I order you in the
   name of Jesus Christ to come out of
   her." And it came out that very hour.

Acts 16:18

The slave girl's testimony was both accurate and
attention-getting. But Paul did not welcome it
because the spirit of divination is not the Holy
Spirit. The first is impersonal publicity that can be
merchandised as a commodity; the second can be
encountered only in a personal meeting. Paul was
right to be annoyed.

What is soothsaying?

PRAYER: Father, make me both wary of talk *about*
you that is only an excuse to keep from meeting
with you, and impatient with religious publicity
that debases your message into an item for pious
gossip. *Amen.*

"Their Hope of Making Money Was Gone"
READ Acts 16:19–24

But when her owners saw that their hope
of making money was gone, they seized
Paul and Silas and dragged them into the
marketplace before the authorities.

Acts 16:19

The slave girl's owners had made it big in the religion business. The girl's psychic gifts were skillfully marketed among people with an appetite for the supernatural. Merchandising religion is still good business. But it is not gospel.

What was "not lawful" (v. 21) in Paul's ministry?

PRAYER: Lord God of grace, continue your great works of deliverance, freeing all your children from exploitive practices that use your good gifts as a means of putting down some in order to enrich others. *Amen.*

"Believe on the Lord Jesus"
READ *Acts* 16:25–40

The jailer called for lights, and rushing in,
  he fell down trembling before Paul and
  Silas. Then he brought them outside and
  said, "Sirs, what must I do to be saved?"
                                    Acts 16:29–30

The prison darkness designed to quarantine the
Christian disease was, instead, incubation for the
seeds of the kingdom. And the prison cell constructed to isolate destructive elements from the
community, in fact, introduced the event of salvation into it.

How did Paul use his Roman citizenship?

PRAYER: "Where can I go from your spirit? Or
where can I flee from your presence?   If I say,
'Surely the darkness shall cover me, and the light
around me become night,' even the darkness is
not dark to you; the night is as bright as the day,
for darkness is as light to you" (Psalm 139:7,
11–12). *Amen.*

"Thessalonica"

READ *Acts* 17:1–9

After Paul and Silas had passed through
Amphipolis and Apollonia, they came to
Thessalonica, where there was a
synagogue of the Jews.

Acts 17:1

For those who like things the way they are—those
who are comfortable in their sins, who enjoy
power at the expense of the weak and indulge lux-
uries in defiance of the poor—the preaching of
the gospel is a threat, not a promise.

What has the gospel displaced in your life?

PRAYER: I praise you, great God, for a gospel that
changes things at the center, that overthrows evil
at the source, that turns the world upside down
and makes all things new, in and through Jesus
Christ, my Lord and Savior. *Amen.*

"Beroea"

READ *Acts* 17:10–15

That very night the believers sent Paul and
Silas off to Beroea; and when they arrived,
they went to the Jewish synagogue.

Acts 17:10

Alexander Whyte, a Scots pastor, said that there
were two ways to read scripture, the way a lawyer
reads a will and the way an heir reads a will. The
Beroean believers quite obviously were reading
it as heirs—with curiosity, eagerness, and application.

How do you read scripture?

PRAYER: Thank you, God, for your scripture, so
rich in truth, so expansive with grace. May everything I read become something that I also live, in
believing obedience and faithful praise. *Amen.*

"Athens"

> While Paul was waiting for them in
> Athens, he was deeply distressed to see
> that the city was full of idols.
>
> *Acts* 17:16

Athens, a center for Greek culture, was littered with the remnants of fatigued philosophy and superstitious religion. The town square was a melting pot where religious and philosophical dilettantes talked incessantly about the gods none of them believed in.

Why was Paul in Athens?

PRAYER: Purge my soul of Athenian curiosities, O Christ—the interest in religion that always manages to avoid worship of God, and the skill in asking questions that never has time to listen to an answer. *Amen.*

"In Front of the Areopagus"
READ *Acts* 17:22–27

Then Paul stood in front of the Areopagus
and said, "Athenians, I see how extremely
religious you are in every way."

Acts 17:22

The gospel can find common ground with any
person. Even in the junkyard of wrecked religions
that was Athens, Paul found some parts that he
could use to make a vehicle for the preaching of
the gospel.

What "common ground" did Paul use?

PRAYER: Lord, grant that I may be neither intimi-
dated by the brilliance of agnostic intellects nor
contemptuous of pagan unbelief. Help me to be
(like Paul) at ease among all people and confident
in conversation with them, knowing that there is
common need among us and a single salvation for
us. *Amen.*

"God's Offspring"

READ *Acts* 17:28–29

"Since we are God's offspring, we ought
not to think that the deity is like gold, or
silver, or stone, an image formed by the
art and imagination of mortals."

Acts 17:29

Paul appeals to common sense. God, if he is to
be at all credible, has to be more than we are, not
less. We derive from him, not he from us. Once
we see this, all the idols, regardless of their size or
beauty, go on the scrap heap.

What is the great appeal of idols, anyway?

PRAYER: Lord God, stretch my imagination to take
in more of the immensity of your being, the ex-
pansiveness of your grace, so that believing in you
becomes an enlargement of my life, not a reduc-
tion of it. *Amen.*

"Now He Commands"

READ *Acts* 17:30–31

"While God has overlooked the times of
human ignorance, now he commands all
people everywhere to repent. . . ."

Acts 17:30

The gospel is not an examination of our past behavior on the basis of which we are either ap-
proved or condemned; it is an invitation to move
from thinking about God to believing in him.

What were "the times of human ignorance"?

PRAYER: Holy Spirit of God, use all my past to
make this present a moment of believing adoration. Gather the ignorance of my thinking and the
wandering of my seeking, and construct a life of
resurrection purpose in me. For Jesus' sake. *Amen.*

OCTOBER 31

"Became Believers"
READ Acts 17:32–34

But some of them joined him and became
believers, including Dionysius the
Areopagite and a woman named
Damaris, and others with them.

Acts 17:34

After Paul plowed the rocky field of Athens and
sowed the seed of the word, the Holy Spirit
brought a harvest. The mockery of some, the curiosity of others, and the commitment of a few—
these are reminiscent of the soils described by
Jesus as different ways of responding to God
(Mark 4:1–9).

Compare these responses to those after Peter's
sermon on the day of Pentecost (Acts 2:12–13).

PRAYER: God of the hundredfold harvest, give me
a listening ear, receptive to your truth and responsive to your love, so that the word you place in my
life may bear daily fruit in works of righteousness.
Amen.

"Tentmakers"

READ *Acts 18:1–4*

. . and, because he was of the same trade,
he stayed with them, and they worked
together—by trade they were
tentmakers.

Acts 18:3

Paul, Aquila, and Priscilla all worked and worshiped together. In the tentmaking shop and synagogue they articulated lives of faith and witness.
Is your work also the place of your witness?

PRAYER: God, you have given me good work to do. Forge a strong link between my place of work and my place of worship, so that what I do with my mind and hands and what I do with my prayers and praise may be coordinated to your glory, through Jesus Christ. *Amen.*

NOVEMBER 2

"A Year and Six Months"

READ Acts 18:5–11

He stayed there a year and six months,
  teaching the word of God among them.

Acts 18:11

What could have been a retreat (the move from synagogue to house) was, in fact, an advance—a sally into gentile territory that resulted in the Corinthian church, one of the most interesting of the first-century churches. Paul's two letters to that congregation document the intensity and liveliness with which they embraced the faith.

What do you know about the church at Corinth?

PRAYER: God, your grace is a lever that uses obstructions as fulcrums to move mountains. All praise to your merciful power! *Amen.*

"Gallio Paid No Attention"

READ Acts 18:12–17

Then all of them seized Sosthenes, the
official of the synagogue, and beat him
in front of the tribunal. But Gallio paid
no attention to any of these things.

Acts 18:17

Gallio, whose name appears on an old stone un-
covered by archaeologists at Corinth, refused to
be drawn into the dispute between Jews and
Christians. His administrative mind could see
no significance in the "questions about words"
(v. 15), which were in fact matters of eternal salvation (and still are).

What issues were at stake between Jews and
Christians?

PRAYER: God of all life, help me to be alert to
everything that happens, to be aware of your presence in the mundane, to be alive to the significance of the trivial; in Jesus' name. *Amen.*

NOVEMBER 4

"If God Wills"
READ *Acts* 18:18–21

> When they asked him to stay longer, he
> declined; but on taking leave of them, he
> said, "I will return to you, if God wills."
> Then he set sail from Ephesus.
>
> *Acts* 18:20–21

Paul's travels were no mere adventuring or pious
wanderlust. His itinerary was willed by God for
the establishment of the church. Far more important than Paul's quick mind and audacious courage was his sensitive responsiveness to the divine
leading.

Why was it important for Paul to travel?

PRAYER: Lead me, Father, to do this day what you
will: to obey the commands of love, to speak the
words of truth, to serve with the compassion of
my Lord. "I do not ask to see The distant scene—
one step enough for me" (John Henry Newman,
"Lead, Kindly Light"). *Amen.*

"Strengthening All the Disciples"
READ *Acts* 18:22–23

After spending some time there he
  departed and went from place to place
  through the region of Galatia and
  Phrygia, strengthening all the disciples.

Acts 18:23

There was nothing haphazard or irresponsible about Paul. His ministry was not a flash-in-the-pan charisma. He not only sowed the seed of the word; he did the patient work of cultivating growing Christians.

Are you better at beginning things than completing them?

PRAYER: Father, give me as much concern for the continuation of your work as for its initiation. I need zest for sprints of witness; I also need stamina for the long-distance run through faith's middle age. *Amen.*

"An Eloquent Man"

> Now there came to Ephesus a Jew named
> Apollos, a native of Alexandria. He was
> an eloquent man, well-versed in the
> scriptures.
>
> *Acts* 18:24

Apollos, gifted with Alexandrian eloquence, was
not too proud to be instructed by the tentmakers
Aquila and Priscilla. His human skill with words
was thereby completed with the divine wisdom
and power of the Holy Spirit.

Why was the "baptism of John" adequate (v. 25)?

PRAYER: What do I lack, dear God? Whom will
you use to develop my ministry? How will you
increase your effectiveness in my life? I give myself to you for instruction and discipline. *Amen.*

"Did You Receive the Holy Spirit?"

READ Acts 19:1–7

> He said to them, "Did you receive the Holy
> Spirit when you became believers?"
> They replied, "No, we have not even
> heard that there is a Holy Spirit."
>
> *Acts 19:2*

Knowledge *about* Jesus Christ is never complete until it becomes knowledge in Christ. That which is in the mind must become an experience in the heart. The gift of the Holy Spirit is that operation by which God becomes a presence within us, bringing gifts of joy, love, and peace.

Read Galatians 5 for a summary of the Spirit's fruits in us.

PRAYER: "Spirit of God, descend upon my heart; Wean it from earth; through all its pulses move; Stoop to my weakness, mighty as Thou art, And make me love Thee as I ought to love" (George Croly, "Spirit of God, Descend upon My Heart"). *Amen.*

"Stubbornly Refused to Believe"
READ *Acts* 19:8–10

When some stubbornly refused to believe
and spoke evil of the Way before the
congregation, he left them, taking the
disciples with him, and argued daily in
the lecture hall of Tyrannus.

Acts 19:9

An effective presentation of the gospel message
is no guarantee of its success. Better methods of
communication will not ensure a response of
faith. Stubbornness of heart, not ineptness in witness, is behind most unbelief.

Why did Paul always start out in the synagogue?

PRAYER: God in Christ, forgive me for my moods
of stubbornness and my acts of disbelief. Shake
my moorings in synagogue routines; jar me loose
from complacencies in well-known scriptures;
break new light from your Word, and bring me
to fresh faith by your faithfulness, "new every
morning" (Lamentations 3:23). *Amen.*

"Itinerant Jewish Exorcists"
READ Acts 19:11–20

> Then some itinerant Jewish exorcists tried
> to use the name of the Lord Jesus over
> those who had evil spirits, saying, "I
> adjure you by the Jesus whom Paul
> proclaims."
>
> *Acts 19:13*

An interest in the supernatural is not, in itself, a
relationship with God. Much of our lust for the
supernatural is only a greedy attempt to exploit
divine power for purposes of entertainment or
ambition.

What were the motives of the sons of Sceva?

PRAYER: Protect me, God of glory, from efforts to
manipulate your power for what I want for myself, and keep me open to the outpouring of your
power that brings to pass what you determine is
good for me; in the name of Jesus. *Amen.*

"Resolved in the Spirit"

READ *Acts* 19:21–22

> Now after these things had been
>   accomplished, Paul resolved in the Spirit
>   to go through Macedonia and Achaia, and
>   then to go on to Jerusalem. He said, "After
>   I have gone there, I must also see Rome."
>
> *Acts* 19:21

These quiet asides show Paul more attentive to his relationship with the Spirit than to the progress of his missionary endeavors. His plans (for he did make plans) were conceived in prayer and carried out in humility.

How do you make your plans?

PRAYER: As I make plans, O God, let your Spirit shape all my motives and direct all my purposes. Help me to be always ready to respond to the next thing you have for me to do. *Amen.*

"Demetrius"

READ *Acts* 19:23–27

A man named Demetrius, a silversmith
    who made silver shrines of Artemis,
    brought no little business to the artisans.
These he gathered together, with the
    workers of the same trade, and said,
    "Men, you know that we get our wealth
    from this business."

Acts 19:24–25

Demetrius had the best reasons for opposing the
preaching of the gospel—he knew that it would
completely change the way in which he made his
living. What he didn't know was that the change
would be for the better, not for the worse.

What difference does the gospel make to the
way you earn your living?

PRAYER: Father, I greatly fear the influences of the
world's gods and goddesses on my life—deities of
money and of lust. Protect me from their power
and help me to conduct my daily affairs under the
banner of redemptive love, as revealed in Jesus
Christ. *Amen.*

"Great Is Artemis of the Ephesians!"
READ Acts 19:28–41

> When they heard this, they were enraged
> and shouted, "Great is Artemis of the
> Ephesians!"
>
> Acts 19:28

The Ephesian riot is an affront to reason and to order. People insecure in their faith are liable to frenzy in defending it. Those who have the flimsiest grounds for their way of life are often the loudest in defending it.

Do you know anyone whose religious enthusiasm is like that of the Artemis worshipers?

PRAYER: Dear Lord, I know that I will be judged not by how much noise I make on your behalf, but by how much love I can share in your name. Lead me to mature witness that gives consistent and convincing evidence of your salvation. In Jesus' name. *Amen.*

"After the Uproar"

> After the uproar had ceased, Paul sent for
> the disciples; and after encouraging
> them and saying farewell, he left for
> Macedonia.

Acts 20:1

The Ephesian riot and the Greek plot, representa-
tive of some of the difficulties of discipleship, do
not divert or deter Paul and his companions. They
never supposed, as some of us do, that Christian
pilgrimage was a sightseeing tour through quiet,
country lanes.

What difficulties do you face in your Christian
walk?

PRAYER. I thank you, dear God, for companions in
discipleship who are willing to face the tests and
temptations that come to all who travel the way of
faith, who do not turn back, and who by their
resolute hope encourage me in faithfulness. *Amen.*

"Eutychus"

READ *Acts* 20:7–12

A young man named Eutychus, who was
sitting in the window, began to sink off
into a deep sleep while Paul talked still
longer. Overcome by sleep, he fell to the
ground three floors below and was
picked up dead.

Acts 20:9

We remember Paul's stay at Troas by what he did
rather than by what he said (even though he
preached all night). His farsighted vision of a
world in need of the gospel did not blind him
to one person's immediate need for a compassionate, healing embrace.

Have you ever been a Eutychus in church?

PRAYER: Father, grant that in my concern for truth
I may never lose sight of the people around me
and their needs. I would hate to get so caught up
in the "big issues" that I offended even one of
"these little ones" (Matthew 18:6). *Amen.*

NOVEMBER 15

"Set Sail"

READ Acts 20:13–16

We went ahead to the ship and set sail for
Assos, intending to take Paul on board
there; for he had made this arrangement,
intending to go by land himself.

Acts 20:13

Paul's travels are part of a vast missionary effort,
continuing into the present, by which communities that have been separated by sin discover in
God's saving love a power that transcends geography and reconnects the family ties of God's
people.

In how many states and countries do you have
Christian friends?

PRAYER: God, as I move from place to place today,
greeting people with your joy and blessing them
with your peace, use me as a means of bringing to
reality your will that "they may all be one" (John
17:21a). In Jesus' name and for his sake. *Amen.*

"I Commend You to God"

"And now I commend you to God and to
the message of his grace, a message that
is able to build you up and to give you
the inheritance among all who are
sanctified."

Acts 20:32

Paul's valediction tells a story of an apostolic life
lived passionately for God among God's people.
God's will, God's love, God's grace are the fixed
points in a career of adventurous humility, compassionate preaching, and alert intelligence.

What do you learn about Paul from this farewell?

PRAYER: Dear God, I thank you for the lives of
your servants who have lived life to the hilt: who
have followed your commands of love unswervingly and who have walked in the footsteps of our
Lord and Savior with joyful courage. *Amen.*

NOVEMBER 17

"Knelt Down"
READ *Acts* 20:36–38

When he had finished speaking, he knelt
down with them all and prayed.

Acts 20:36

Christian community is conceived and nurtured
in an ambience of prayer, God being partner and
presence in all our exchanges of truth and affec-
tion. The poignancy of Paul's leave-taking is evidence of his loving involvement with the Ephesian
Christians.

What did Paul mean to these people?

PRAYER: God, when the time comes, help me to
release friends and family to your leading, remembering that there is "a time to seek, and a
time to lose; a time to keep, and a time to throw
away" (Ecclesiastes 3:6). *Amen.*

"Knelt Down on the Beach"
READ *Acts* 21:1–6

When our days there were ended, we left
and proceeded on our journey; and all
of them, with wives and children,
escorted us outside the city. There we
knelt down on the beach and prayed and
said farewell to one another. Then we
went on board the ship, and they
returned home.

Acts 21:5–6

Any place is the proper place to pray; wherever
Christians kneel in the vast cathedral of creation,
altars appear unbidden. There can be few places left
on earth that have not been consecrated by someone's prayers, whether formal or spontaneous.

Where are some of the significant places you
have prayed?

PRAYER: Wherever I am today, O God—in car,
kitchen, school, office, workroom—I will make it
a place of prayer. As I bend or bow my head, meet
me in the power of your Spirit and lead me in the
way of your salvation. In Jesus' name. *Amen.*

"Agabus"

READ *Acts* 21:7–16

> While we were staying there for several days, a prophet named Agabus came down from Judea. He came to us and took Paul's belt, bound his own feet and hands with it, and said, "Thus says the Holy Spirit, 'This is the way the Jews in Jerusalem will bind the man who owns this belt and will hand him over to the Gentiles.'"

Acts 21:10–11

Undeterred by the ominous prophecy of Agabus, Paul steadily set his course for Jerusalem. The question for Paul was never, "How can I prolong my life?" but always, "How can I obey my Lord?"

Compare this incident with what Paul wrote in Philippians 3:13–14.

PRAYER: "Lead us, O Father, to Thy heavenly rest, However rough and steep the pathway be, Through joy or sorrow, as Thou deemest best, Until our lives are perfected in Thee" (William Henry Burleigh, "Lead Us, O Father, in the Paths of Peace"). *Amen.*

"Purified Himself"

READ *Acts* 21:17–26

Then Paul took the men, and the next day,
having purified himself, he entered the
temple with them, making public the
completion of the days of purification
when the sacrifice would be made for
each of them.

Acts 21:26

Paul, a fierce champion of the liberty of others,
readily gave up his personal prerogatives when he
thought doing so would make belief easier for
another. The difficulties of some Jews in making
the transition from Moses to Jesus were eased by
his considerateness.

Why were the Jerusalem Jews wary of Paul?

PRAYER: Help me, dear God, to use the freedom
you have given me in ways that neither offend the
conscience of others nor distract from the life of
the gospel. I want the considerations of your love,
not the demands for my rights, to shape the freedom in which Christ has made me free. *Amen.*

NOVEMBER 21

"Away with Him!"

READ *Acts* 21:27–36

The crowd that followed kept shouting,
 "Away with him!"

Acts 21:36

Accepting Jesus as Messiah, and accepting Gentiles as brothers and sisters in faith, seemed to many Jews to be the first step in destroying their way of life. Angry fear blinded them to the reality that this was the final stage in fulfilling their God-ordained mission.

How is this similar to the mob rejection of Jesus?

PRAYER: God Almighty, you know how frequently I misunderstand and misinterpret the work and witness of others. I am quick to react and vehement in my rejections. Help me, instead, to offer up to you that which doesn't fit my expectations and faithfully pray that your will may be done. Amen.

"Listen to the Defense"
READ Acts 21:37–22:2

"Brothers and fathers, listen to the defense
that I now make before you."

Acts 22:1

Caught in a cross fire of Jewish anger ("Away with
him!") and Roman misunderstanding ("Are you
not the Egyptian?"), Paul clarifies his position. A
remarkably clear witness to the gospel is pub-
lished under the stress of accusation and hostility.

Why did Paul's use of Hebrew catch the crowd's
attention?

PRAYER: All times are in your hands, Lord, and all
of them equally useful for accomplishing your
will. I will welcome times of crisis along with seasons of serenity, the moments of enmity along
with the hours of acceptance, as occasions for
receiving your strength and sharing your grace.
Amen.

NOVEMBER 23

"I Am a Jew"

READ *Acts* 22:3–21

"I am a Jew, born in Tarsus in Cilicia, but
brought up in this city at the feet of
Gamaliel, educated strictly according to
our ancestral law, being zealous for God,
just as all of you are today."

Acts 22:3

What God, not mortals, did in Paul's life was de-
cisive. What God said to him, not what people
said about him, was formative. As Paul speaks, his
story comes out not as entertaining autobiogra-
phy but as compelling witness.

What are two or three important events in your
life?

PRAYER: In gratitude I sort through the memories
of your lordship, O God. I recall times when I
realized your saving love; I remember moments
when I sensed your guidance into new paths of
obedience. Thank you for endless mercy and
grace abounding, through Jesus Christ. *Amen.*

"A Roman Citizen"
READ *Acts* 22:22–29

But when they had tied him up with thongs,
Paul said to the centurion who was
standing by, "Is it legal for you to flog a
Roman citizen who is uncondemned?"

Acts 22:25

As in Philippi so in Jerusalem, Roman citizenship conferred certain rights that Paul used to protect himself from the irrational anger of the mob. In such a way the secular order was put to the use of a gospel witness.

Compare this appeal to Roman rights with that in Acts 16:37–39.

PRAYER: I pray, Father, for the leaders in my government. Use them to preserve the orders of justice in which your will may be done and your kingdom come; for Jesus' sake, to whom be the power and the glory forever. *Amen.*

"You Whitewashed Wall!"

READ *Acts* 22:30–23:5

> Then the high priest Ananias ordered those standing near him to strike him on the mouth. At this Paul said to him, "God will strike you, you whitewashed wall! Are you sitting there to judge me according to the law, and yet in violation of the law you order me to be struck?"
>
> *Acts* 23:2–3

Ananias's high priestly robes barely concealed his contempt for justice. And Paul, infuriated by the hypocrisy, exploded in anger. He had been treated far better by the civil authorities of Rome than by the religious leaders of Judaism.

Compare Jesus' denunciation of hypocrisy in Matthew 23:27–28.

PRAYER: Holy God, I want my every attitude and action to flow out of my love for you and my knowledge of your will, even as that love and knowledge are revealed to me in Jesus Christ. *Amen.*

"The Lord Stood Near Him"
READ *Acts* 23:6–11

That night the Lord stood near him and
said, "Keep up your courage! For just as
you have testified for me in Jerusalem,
so you must bear witness also in Rome."

Acts 23:11

It is plausible to imagine the beleaguered apostle
with this psalm-prayer on his lips: "O grant us
help against the foe, for human help is worthless.
With God we shall do valiantly; it is he who will
tread down our foes" (Psalm 108:12–13).

In what time of need has God provided you
with courage and strength?

PRAYER: "I fear no foe, with Thee at hand to bless:
Ills have no weight, and tears no bitterness.
Where is death's sting? Where, grave, thy victory?
I triumph still, if Thou abide with me" (Henry F.
Lyte, "Abide with Me: Fast Falls the Eventide").
Amen.

"Ready to Do Away with Him"

READ *Acts* 23:12–15

"Now then, you and the council must
   notify the tribune to bring him down to
   you, on the pretext that you want to
   make a more thorough examination of
   his case. And we are ready to do away
   with him before he arrives."

Acts 23:15

It is the sheerest naïveté to suppose that goodness
will be rewarded in this world or righteousness
acclaimed, for very frequently they provoke hate
and hostility. Following the will of God is not a
strategy for success in the world.

Read what Jesus said on this subject in Matthew
5:10–11.

PRAYER: Lord Jesus Christ, you unswervingly took
the way of the cross and accepted the rejection
of those you came to love; you loved your enemies and those who despitefully used you. Grant
courage that I may follow in your steps. *Amen.*

"Ambush"

READ *Acts* 23:16–22

Now the son of Paul's sister heard about
the ambush; so he went and gained
entrance to the barracks and told Paul.

Acts 23:16

It is possible that Paul's bitterest enemies were
from his own family, which would account for
his nephew's knowledge of the death plot. Un-
daunted, Paul experienced what a psalmist sang:
"If my father and mother forsake me, the LORD
will take me up" (Psalm 27:10).

Read Psalm 27 as a message to Paul in trouble.

PRAYER: "Teach me your way, O LORD, and lead
me on a level path because of my enemies. Do not
give me up to the will of my adversaries, for false
witnesses have risen against me, and they are
breathing out violence. I believe that I shall see the
goodness of the LORD in the land of the living"
(Psalm 27:11–13). *Amen.*

NOVEMBER 29

"Safely to Felix"
READ *Acts* 23:23–30

"Also provide mounts for Paul to ride, and
   take him safely to Felix the governor."

Acts 23:24

A military escort of 470 soldiers, horsemen, and
spearmen for God's servant! The whole military
machinery of Rome is set in motion and put to
the purposes of God's providence.

How does your government serve God's purposes?

PRAYER: Righteous God, while I live among the
kingdoms of this earth I will pray for peace. Use
the ordinary structures of government and the
common principles of justice to protect your servants and advance your ways until "thy kingdom
come." *Amen.*

"Under Guard in Herod's Headquarters"
READ Acts 23:31–35

. . . he said, "I will give you a hearing
when your accusers arrive." Then he
ordered that he be kept under guard in
Herod's headquarters.

Acts 23:35

Paul never seems to have regarded his imprison-
ments as disasters. In prison he praised God,
witnessed to his guards, and wrote some of the
letters that have become an important part of our
scriptures.

What is the worst thing that happened to you
in the year past? How did God use it to "the praise
of his glory"? (Ephesians 2:14)

PRAYER: Praise your great name, Almighty God. I
thank you for all the dark days when I thought I
was at the end of my rope and then found myself
secure in your protective hand, saved by your
grace in Jesus Christ, to whom be glory forever
and ever. *Amen.*

"An Agitator"

READ Acts 24:1–9

"We have, in fact, found this man a
pestilent fellow, an agitator among all
the Jews throughout the world, and a
ringleader of the sect of the Nazarenes."

Acts 24:5

The charges were accurate; only the perspective
was askew. The agitation of which Tertullus com-
plained was a healthy stirring in the stagnant
religious waters. Christopher Fry describes the
phenomenon positively: "The frozen misery /
of centuries breaks, cracks, begins to move, / The
thunder of the floes, / The thaw, the flood, the
upstart Spring" ("A Sleep of Prisoners," in *Three
Plays* [New York: Oxford Univ. Press, 1961],
p. 209).

Summarize Tertullus's accusation.

PRAYER: When habits get in the way of obedience,
or traditions in the way of trust, prod me to fresh
faith by your Spirit. Move broodingly and creatively over me, O God, stirring me to new life in
Christ. *Amen.*

DECEMBER 2

"According to the Way"
READ *Acts* 24:10–16

"But this I admit to you, that according
    to the Way, which they call a sect, I
    worship the God of our ancestors,
    believing everything laid down
    according to the law or written in the
    prophets."

Acts 24:14

A prominent aspect of Christian experience is the
realization that Jesus is the Main Road, the Way, to
God; and that all other roads are either access
lanes eventually leading to faith, detours avoiding
faith, or falsely marked routes "leading to destruc-
tion" (Matthew 7:13).

Compare Acts 9:2 for similar terminology.

PRAYER: Blessed God, help me to be one of those
people "who do not follow the advice of the
wicked, or take the path that sinners tread, or sit
in the seat of scoffers" (Psalm 1:1). I will, this day,
delight in your word and accept "the way, and the
truth, and the life" (John 14:6) in Jesus. *Amen.*

"It Is About the Resurrection"
READ Acts 24:17–21

"Or let these men here tell what crime they
    had found when I stood before the
    council, unless it was this one sentence
    that I called out while standing before
    them, 'It is about the resurrection of the
    dead that I am on trial before you today.'"
Acts 24:20–21

From the mass of custom and opinion making up
what people call "religion," arguments and disputes issue endlessly. Paul cuts through the under-
brush and lays open the central issue: Will we
argue over our ideas of God, or will we respond to
God's gift of life that is resurrection?

Why does Paul take this stand on the resurrection?

PRAYER: Lord Jesus Christ, be risen and reign in
me today! Bring all the promises of resurrection
to fulfillment in my body and I will walk, by your
grace, in newness of life. Amen.

"Felix"

> But Felix, who was rather well informed
> about the Way, adjourned the hearing
> with the comment, "When Lysias the
> tribune comes down, I will decide
> your case."

Acts 24:22

Procrastination is the most urbane of responses to the gospel. It is knowledgeable ("rather well informed"); it is well intentioned ("when Lysias . . . comes down, I will decide"); it is courteous ("ordered . . . let him have some liberty"; v. 23). But for all its show of courtesy, it is still, at bottom, a rejection.

What word from God have you put off dealing with?

PRAYER: God in Christ, quick in mercy and swift in love, cure my moral reflexes of sluggishness and rouse my desultory spirit from sloth, keeping me alert and responsive to you through the hours of this day. *Amen.*

DECEMBER 5

"After Two Years Had Passed"
READ Acts 24:24–27

After two years had passed, Felix was
  succeeded by Porcius Festus; and since
  he wanted to grant the Jews a favor, Felix
  left Paul in prison.

Acts 24:27

Felix sat through the most protracted "altar call"
on record. For two years he hesitated, manufac-
tured excuses, and pretended to be making up his
mind. Conversations with Paul about the faith
were stimulating and frequent, but the time for
decision, the "convenient moment" (v. 25, Phillips
Translation), never came.

How many different motives operate at cross-
purposes in Felix?

PRAYER: I seize this very moment, dear Lord, to
receive your word, to hope in your promises, to
love your commands, and to step out in obedience in the way of the cross. *Amen.*

DECEMBER 6

"Festus"

READ *Acts* 25:1–5

Three days after Festus had arrived in the
province, he went up from Caesarea to
Jerusalem where the chief priests and
the leaders of the Jews gave him a report
against Paul.

Acts 25:1–2a

Paul's case, shelved by Felix, was, at the insti-
gation of the Jerusalem leaders, revived before
Festus, the new governor. But it was murder, not
justice, that motivated them. Having little hope of
winning the case against Paul in court, they laid
plans to assassinate him from ambush.

What is your impression of Festus?

PRAYER: Mighty God, I know how trivial are the
machinations of the wicked and how futile the
cunning of the evil in your sight. Why then am I
frightened by their bluster and boasts? Restore my
confidence in your lordship and bless me with
your peace. *Amen.*

"I Appeal to the Emperor"
READ Acts 25:6–12

> "Now if I am in the wrong and have
> committed something for which I
> deserve to die, I am not trying to escape
> death; but if there is nothing to their
> charges against me, no one can turn me
> over to them. I appeal to the emperor."
>
> Acts 25:11

After two years in the Caesarean prison, Paul is restless to continue his missionary journey. The opportunity presents itself in an appeal to the emperor. The Romans, who had kept him alive from assassination attempts by his compatriots, will now pay his passage to Rome so he can preach the gospel there.

How does Paul use his Roman citizenship to further his ministry?

PRAYER: "Enfolded deep in Thy dear love, Held in Thy law, I stand; Thy hand in all things I behold, And all things in Thy hand; Thou leadest me by unsought ways, And turnest my mourning into praise" (Samuel Longfellow, "I Look to Thee in Every Need"). Amen.

"Paul's Case"

READ *Acts 25:13–22*

Since they were staying there several days,
Festus laid Paul's case before the king,
saying, "There is a man here who was
left in prison by Felix."

Acts 25:14

Festus, supposing that anyone who aroused so much opposition must have committed a serious crime, is puzzled when the charges have to do with a proclamation of life: "Jesus, who had died, but whom Paul asserted to be alive" (v. 19).

Which are more influential—acts of crime or acts of virtue?

PRAYER: God, my mind, littered with the trivial banalities of sin and the gossip of death, needs a good housecleaning; sweep it clean by your grace as I set my mind on the things of the Spirit, all matters of life and peace. *Amen.*

DECEMBER 9

"Prominent Men"
READ *Acts* 25:23–27

So on the next day Agrippa and Bernice
came with great pomp, and they entered
the audience hall with the military
tribunes and the prominent men of the
city. Then Festus gave the order and Paul
was brought in.

Acts 25:23

There is something faintly ludicrous in the pro-
ceedings. Paul is passed from centurion to tribune
to governor to king, and none is acute enough
to understand the case, none energetic enough to
complete the process of justice. But it is not time
wasted, for Paul's ministry penetrates prisons,
courts, and finally, the palace of Caesar.

What do you think was the attitude in the court
to Paul?

PRAYER: In a society more concerned with appearance than reality, help me, Lord, to live in but
not of the world: as salt, my intercessions are a
means of your grace; and as light, my witness an
instance of your love. In and through Jesus Christ.
Amen.

DECEMBER 10

"My Defense"

READ *Acts* 26:1–3

"I consider myself fortunate that it is
   before you, King Agrippa, I am to make
   my defense today against all the
   accusations of the Jews. . . ."

Acts 26:2

Paul's defense is the story of his conversion. It is
told now for the third time (see also Acts 9:11
and 22:3–16). His message is not an elaboration
of ideas about God, but a repeated witness of an
action of God. He himself, an instance of what
God in Christ does, is the data that must be considered.

Read Matthew 10:19.

PRAYER: Lord Jesus Christ, when I am called upon
to give an account of my life, use my words to
speak your will, so that in my speech I may not
just give a point of view, but provide actual evidence of what you do in love and salvation. *Amen.*

"On Account of My Hope"
READ *Acts* 26:4–8

"And now I stand here on trial on account
of my hope in the promise made by God
to our ancestors. . . ."

Acts 26:6

Hebrew history was charged with anticipation:
What would God do next? No other people had
hoped so consistently nor had its hopes realized
in so many actual events. Paul's question is incred-
ulous: Since when has it become criminal in a Jew
to hope that God raises the dead? Why is it supposed incredible that God should do something
we had not clearly calculated?

What does a Christian hope for?

PRAYER: I cannot keep up with what you are
doing, O God. I do not know what you will do
next, only that it will be surprisingly good. So I
hope. Keep me ready for the new things you have
for me today, in Jesus Christ. Amen.

"*Against the Name of Jesus*"
READ *Acts* 26:9–11

"Indeed, I myself was convinced that I
ought to do many things against the
name of Jesus of Nazareth."

Acts 26:9

It is possible for a well-intentioned person to do
evil deeds. Good motives can be directed to
wrong ends. The persecution of Christians was
undertaken by persons, like Paul, of high moral
character and impressive intelligence.

Why did Paul tell about his earlier opposition
to Christians?

PRAYER: I put my confidence, merciful God, not
in what I know nor in what I intend, but in you to
"work in me that which is well pleasing in your
sight," through Jesus Christ, my Lord and Savior.
Amen.

"Light"

READ *Acts* 26:12–18

". . . when at midday along the road, your
Excellency, I saw a light from heaven,
brighter than the sun, shining around
me and my companions."

Acts 26:13

God's revelation is an explosion of light. When
the first-day words "Let there be light" (Genesis
1:3) are personalized in a meeting with Jesus
Christ, the "light of the world" (John 8:12), we
clearly see who God is, who we are, and where
we are going.

What is the function of light in your life?

PRAYER: "Christ, whose glory fills the skies; Christ,
the only Light, Sun of Righteousness, arise, Triumph o'er the shades of night; Dayspring from
on high, be near; Daystar, in my heart appear"
(Charles Wesley, "Christ, Whose Glory Fills the
Skies"). Amen.

"Not Disobedient"
READ *Acts* 26:19–23

"After that, King Agrippa, I was not
disobedient to the heavenly vision."

Acts 26:19

The blazing light of God's saving love in Jesus
Christ is not a show to entertain us. Christians are
not spectators with box seats at the Revelation, but
those who, when the will and ways of God become visible, believingly embrace his will and
obediently walk in his way.

What did Paul learn in the vision?

PRAYER: God, I don't want scraps of vision or
fragments of insight lying around and gathering
dust in my heart. Forbid that I should be unresponsive or disobedient to any of what you have
so graciously and clearly made known of your
love and purpose for me in Jesus Christ. *Amen.*

DECEMBER 15

"Not Out of My Mind"
READ *Acts* 26:24–26

> But Paul said, "I am not out of my mind,
> most excellent Festus, but I am speaking
> the sober truth."
>
> *Acts* 26:25

Christian faith is not a private wish-fulfillment dream or a psychotic hallucination. It is life lived in response to the reliably reported event of God revealed in Jesus Christ.

Has anyone ever accused you of being crazy for being a Christian?

PRAYER: Thank you, gracious Father, for the solid, verified reality of Jesus Christ, crucified "under Pontius Pilate" and raised to new life "in accordance with the scriptures" (1 Corinthians 15:4). Amen.

"So Quickly Persuading Me?"
READ Acts 26:27–29

Agrippa said to Paul, "Are you so quickly
persuading me to become a Christian?"
Acts 26:28

How long did Agrippa want? He was already con-
versant with the long story of salvation as it had
come down through Israel, and he now had the
clearest of witnesses standing before him, providing the evidence for God's life-changing love and
eternity-shaping power.

Do you procrastinate?

PRAYER: Today is the day, O God. I know that.
Help me to act on your command-promises, re-
ceiving right now all that you intend for me, in
Jesus Christ. *Amen.*

"If"

READ *Acts* 26:30–32

Agrippa said to Festus, "This man could
have been set free if he had not appealed
to the emperor."

Acts 26:32

Agrippa concluded, after his examination, that the
appeal to Caesar was a mistake; it would only prolong the already drawn-out process of justice.
What he didn't know was the reason that Paul was
going to Rome: not to get a trial but to get a pulpit for proclaiming the gospel at the center of the
Western world.

What might have happened if Paul had not
gone to Rome?

PRAYER: Give me the skill, all wise God, to read
the meaning of events in the light of your purposes and in the confidence of your love, and so
find cause to praise your name in everything, in
Jesus' name. *Amen.*

"His Friends"

READ *Acts* 27:1–3

> The next day we put in at Sidon; and Julius
> treated Paul kindly, and allowed him to
> go to his friends to be cared for.
>
> *Acts* 27:3

Paul was blessed on ship and in port with good friends. In Sidon his friends fortified him after the ordeal of prison in Caesarea; later, Aristarchus and Luke would be his companions on the perilous sea voyage to Rome.

What friends are used by God to enrich your life?

PRAYER: Thank you, dear God, for friends who lighten burdens, deepen joys, and expand my life in the resurrection fellowship of your love. Especially I thank you for . . . [name as many friends as you wish]. *Amen.*

"An Alexandrian Ship"

READ *Acts* 27:4–8

There the centurion found an Alexandrian
ship bound for Italy and put us on
board.

Acts 27:6

The ship was one of a large fleet devoted to trans-
porting wheat from Egypt, the granary of Rome,
to Italy. The economic importance of the ship,
significant as it was, did not compare with its
missionary importance.

Read Acts 27:38 for a description of the cargo.

PRAYER: I marvel, O God, at how you put everything—the weather, the seas, ships and sailors—
to work in bringing about your purposes,
working "in everything . . . for good." Praise your
great name! *Amen.*

"Now Dangerous"
READ Acts 27:9–12

> Since much time had been lost and sailing
> was now dangerous, because even the
> Fast had already gone by, Paul advised
> them, saying, "Sirs, I can see that the
> voyage will be with danger and much
> heavy loss, not only of the cargo and the
> ship, but also of our lives."
>
> Acts 27:9–10

The Fast was the Day of Atonement. In the year of this voyage (A.D. 59) it fell on October 5, well into the dangerous season for navigation when northerly winds came up with suddenness, frequency, and violence. The centurion was imprudent not to listen to Paul, a traveler of great experience on both land and sea.

Read 2 Corinthians 11:25–27 for an account of Paul's travels.

PRAYER: Holy Spirit of God, give me the gift of discernment to perceive your will, the gift of boldness to declare it to others, and the gift of patience to quietly persevere when your way is rejected. *Amen.*

DECEMBER 21

"Pounded by the Storm"
READ Acts 27:13–20

We were being pounded by the storm so
violently that on the next day they began
to throw the cargo overboard. . . .

Acts 27:18

The narrative, terse and vivid, conveys every nuance of hope and despair common to the human condition—from strenuous attempts at saving the ship, to helpless abandonment to the ancient chaotic elements of wind and sea.

Get a map and trace the voyage.

PRAYER: "Eternal Father, strong to save, Whose arm doth bind the restless wave, Who biddest the mighty ocean deep Its own appointed limits keep: O hear us when we cry to Thee For those in peril on the sea" (William Whiting, "Eternal Father, Strong to Save"). Amen.

DECEMBER 22

"Keep Up Your Courage"
READ *Acts* 27:21–26

"I urge you now to keep up your courage,
for there will be no loss of life among
you, but only of the ship."

Acts 27:22

Courage! God is in the midst of the storm! His word banishes anxiety and demolishes fear. Salvation is assured even while we continue to experience tribulation.

What do you fear?

PRAYER: Strong God of Jacob, when rough waters tumble me in doubt and thunderous waves shake my confidence, dissolve my terrors, quiet my fears, and firm my faith with your peace, even in Jesus Christ. *Amen.*

DECEMBER 23

"About Midnight"
READ *Acts* 27:27–32

When the fourteenth night had come, as
we were drifting across the sea of Adria,
about midnight the sailors suspected that
they were nearing land.

Acts 27:27

Many, courageous and selfless, followed Paul's
counsel and learned to put their trust in God.
Others, refusing to renounce cowardice and selfishness, thought only of saving their own skins.
Crisis brings out the best in some, the worst in
others.

Have you ever heard a sermon on "the four
anchors"?

PRAYER: Father in heaven, when all supports give
way for me, grant that I may learn to lean on your
everlasting arms. Make the hour of crisis an hour
of grace. *Amen.*

DECEMBER 24

"He Took Bread"
READ *Acts* 27:33–38

After he had said this, he took bread; and
  giving thanks to God in the presence of
  all, he broke it and began to eat.

Acts 27:35

Faced now with the life that God had promised,
not the death that they had feared, the travelers
ended their fast and began eating. The meal was
an act of faith: receiving in gratitude strength for
the life that was to continue for them, by God's
grace.

Why do you think they had not eaten?

PRAYER: "Yours as we stand at this table you set,
yours as we eat the bread our hearts can't forget,
We are the sign of your life with us yet, we are
yours. Take our bread, we ask you; take our
hearts, we love you, take our lives, O Father, we
are yours" (Joseph Wise, "Take Our Bread"). *Amen.*

DECEMBER 25

"Brought Safely to Land"

READ *Acts* 27:39–44

And so it was that all were brought safely
to land.

Acts 27:44b

The shipwreck, as Paul had reassured them earlier
(v. 22), took place without loss of life, but not
without the narrowest of escapes for Paul, whose
Lord had preserved the entire company.

Why were they going to kill the prisoners?

PRAYER: I put my life in your strong and gentle
hands, O Father. Keep me from anxious fears, lead
me in joyful service, bless me with abundant love;
for Jesus' sake. Amen.

"Malta"

READ *Acts* 28:1–6

After we had reached safety, we then
learned that the island was called Malta.

Acts 28:1

The Maltese, warmly hospitable to the bedraggled survivors, were also incredibly superstitious. Paul, in quick succession, was a victim to be helped, a murderer to be feared, and a god to be adored. Faith in Christ would deliver them from such instability and put a foundation of God's steadfast love under their already admirable human compassion.

Where is Malta?

PRAYER: Fix my faith firmly, O God, in your love revealed in Jesus so that I may not be "tossed to and fro . . . by every wind of doctrine" (Ephesians 4:14). Rescue me from groundless fears and misdirected enthusiasms. Put me on a level path, steady in my praise and habitual in my obedience, for Jesus' sake. *Amen.*

"Publius"

READ *Acts* 28:7–10

Now in the neighborhood of that place
were lands belonging to the leading man
of the island, named Publius, who
received us and entertained us hospitably
for three days.

Acts 28:7

When we are attentive to God's leading and responsive to people's needs, there are no interruptions and no delays. Forced to winter in Malta and wait for the safer sailing weather of spring, Paul, eager to get to Rome, could have impatiently paced the beach in frustration. Instead he engaged in a remarkable healing ministry.

How do you treat interruptions?

PRAYER: When my plans are upset, O God, help me to take it as an occasion to get in fresh touch with your will. When interruptions interfere with my timetable, help me to accept that as a signal to renew my trust that "my times are in your hand" (Psalm 31:15). *Amen.*

"And So We Came to Rome"
READ Acts 28:11–16

There we found believers and were invited
to stay with them for seven days. And so
we came to Rome.

Acts 28:14

Three years earlier (in A.D. 57) Paul had written to
the Christians in Rome: ". . . without ceasing I
remember you always in my prayers, asking that
by God's will I may somehow at last succeed in
coming to you. For I am longing to see you so
that I may share with you some spiritual gift to
strengthen you" (Romans 1:9–11). His prayer is
answered.

Why was Rome important to the missionary
task?

PRAYER: God, your answers to my prayers do not
come at the times I demand them or in the ways I
expect them, but they come. Keep me persevering
through circumstances that contradict what I
think is your will, and trusting in times that seem
separated from your purposes. *Amen.*

"Everywhere It Is Spoken Against"
READ Acts 28:17–22

"But we would like to hear from you what
   you think, for with regard to this sect
   we know that everywhere it is spoken
   against."

Acts 28:22

Early in Luke's first volume, Jesus is described as
"a sign that will be opposed" (Luke 2:34). Now
late in the second volume, sixty years later, it is
written that the gospel of Jesus is "spoken against."

Why does the gospel provoke opposition?

PRAYER: Father Almighty, "take every thought
captive to obey Christ" (2 Corinthians 10:5).
Conquer every impulse to disobedience in me;
convert every wayward thought. "Break down
every idol, cast out every foe" (J. Nicholson,
"Whiter Than Snow, Lord" in *Redemptions Songs*
[London: Pickering & Inglis, n.d.], p. 56). *Amen.*

"Some Were Convinced"
READ *Acts* 28:23–28

Some were convinced by what he said,
while others refused to believe.

Acts 28:24

Ministry in Rome began by gathering the Jews—those who "were entrusted with the oracles of God" (Romans 3:2)—and presenting to them the evidence for the messianic lordship of Jesus. The acceptance by some provided a knowledgeable and mature base for Christian community; rejection by others was a stimulus for invading the pagan populace with the good news.

Note how Jesus uses this same quotation from Isaiah in Luke 8:9–10.

PRAYER: "More about Jesus would I know, More of His grace to others show; More of His saving fullness see, More of His love who died for me. More about Jesus, let me learn, More of His holy will discern. Spirit of God, my teacher be, Showing the things of Christ to me" (Eliza E. Hewitt, "More About Jesus Would I Know"). *Amen.*

"Without Hindrance"

READ *Acts* 28:30–31

> He lived there two whole years at his own
> expense and welcomed all who came to
> him, proclaiming the kingdom of God and
> teaching about the Lord Jesus Christ with
> all boldness and without hindrance.
>
> *Acts* 28:30–31

Luke's narrative ends quite differently from what
the enemies of the Christians intended. The last
words, "without hindrance," defy and surprise both
the malice of Jerusalem and the indifference of
Rome. Instead of brooding frustration over delays
in justice, there is an imaginative proclamation of
the unfettered word; instead of a bitterly resented
dead end in a dungeon, an open door into the
whole world.

What do you know of the early church's ex-
pansion?

PRAYER: What will be the last word on me, dear
God? Not, I hope, what I have done or failed to
do, but what you are doing and continue to do.
Use my life and my death for your glory. "Now to
him who by the power at work within us is able
to accomplish abundantly far more than all we can
ask or imagine, to him be glory in the church and
in Christ Jesus to all generations, forever and
ever" (Ephesians 3:20–21). *Amen.*

Topic Index

Scripture Index